Global Training
How to Design a Program for the Multinational Corporation

Sylvia B. Odenwald

THE AMERICAN SOCIETY FOR TRAINING AND DEVELOPMENT
Alexandria, Virginia 22313

BUSINESS ONE IRWIN
Homewood, Illinois 60430

This publication is designed to provide accurate and
authoritative information in regard to the subject matter
covered. It is sold with the understanding that neither the
author nor the publisher is engaged in rendering legal, accounting,
or other professional service. If legal advice or other expert
assistance is required, the services of a competent
professional person should be sought.

*From a Declaration of Principles jointly adopted by a Committee
of the American Bar Association and a Committee of Publishers.*

Sponsoring editor: Cynthia A. Zigmund
Project editor: Jane Lightell
Production manager: Ann Cassady
Jacket designer: Image House, Inc.
Compositor: Montgomery Media, Inc.
Typeface: 11/13 Times Roman
Printer: Arcata Graphics—Kingsport

Library of Congress Cataloging-in-Publication Data

Odenwald, Sylvia B.,
    Global training: how to design a program for the multinational
corporation/Sylvia B. Odenwald
        p.   cm.
    Issued by the American Society for Training and Development.
    Includes bibliographical references and index.
    ISBN 1-55623-986-6
        1. International business enterprises—Employees—Training of—
United States.   I. American Society for Training and Development.
II. Title.
HF5549.5.T7028   1993
658.3'12404—dc20   93–18101

Printed in the United States of America
1 2 3 4 5 6 7 8 9 0 K P 0 9 8 7 6 5 4 3

*This book is dedicated to Wells, Eddie, and Elizabeth Burr;
Bob, Lynn, Cliff, Carol, Edie, Don, and Sally,
Craig, Alana, Christi, and Eric
—who fill my world with love and meaning.*

Contents

Foreword

Globalization, the attempt to bring nations and societies closer together, is a challenging process. Technology can provide a measure of uniformity, although it is constrained by empirical limitations of nature. The human element, on the other hand, is dynamic, changing, and unique to each culture. Given today's concern for addressing such diversity, *Global Training: How to Design a Program for the Multinational Corporation*, is a welcome addition to the human resource library. It is welcome for a number of reasons, the most important of which is the underlying philosophy of providing context-specific solutions to training needs.

At the World Environment Center, designing training programs to fit specific cultures is integral to meeting the pedagogical requirements. Thus, training programs designed in one country should always be redesigned to take into account institutional, political, and social information before presentation in another country. By understanding and contrasting training methods and techniques from country to country, a more durable result is achieved. In this spirit, *Global Training* provides a variety of concepts and techniques which are as appropriate to technology transfer as they are to training. In fact, technology transfer goals often are not met due to training deficiencies.

As a guide for globally-oriented human resource development specialists, *Global Training* succeeds in providing a framework upon which to build culturally-sensitive training programs. Its real contribution will be to alert those of us involved in cross-cultural training to the broader context of our efforts. The author, Sylvia Odenwald, and her contributors, the American Society for Training and Development and its international executive committee of the International Professional Practice Area are to be commended for providing this notable contribution to the global trainer's library.

Antony G. Marcil
President and CEO
World Environment Center
New York, New York

Preface

The Executive Committee of the American Society for Training and Development's (ASTD) International Professional Practice Area (IPPA) has been a valuable resource in helping national ASTD broaden its vision and move toward an international professional society. Members who serve on that Executive Committee, along with national ASTD headquarters staff, have received many requests for assistance in global training issues during the past few years. In fact, it was just such a request that prompted the basic research for this book.

Although I originated the idea for this book and authored it, I have received invaluable assistance from members of the IPPA Executive Committee, key international consultants, and corporate training professionals who have shared information and training program ideas.

Throughout these pages I have provided information and tools on:

- How to assess specific company global training needs.
- The types of courses that address cultural diversity and global issues.
- How training courses can be designed and adapted to company specifics.
- Knowledge and skills the trainer must have to design and present this training.
- How to set up a company training program that is flexible enough to move beyond current to future needs.
- How to enlist help at non-U.S. sites to identify issues that may not be apparent to corporate headquarters in the United States.

This book discusses a training process for multinational corporations. *Multinational* simply means that the firm is conducting business and working in multiple countries. Although the activities in designing a global training process sometimes overlap, the chapters are arranged sequentially to reflect the steps in the process:

1. Assessing global training needs.

2. Assisting management to think globally.

3. Creating a global training strategy.

4. Designing guidelines for global training.

5. Developing a global training curriculum.

6. Selecting and training global managers and trainers

7. Managing a multinational training system.

Global Training is written with four main groups in mind:

1. American human resource directors, managers, and trainers in large, midsized, or small companies.

2. Human resource consultants who want to assist their client-base with cross-cultural issues.

3. University human resource development professors and students.

4. Human resource directors, managers, and trainers in other countries.

Global Training is a guide for corporate training managers in multinational corporations headquartered in the United States who face the dilemma: "What do we do? Where do we begin?" I sincerely trust this book will assist companies to begin a development process with a more comprehensive approach to global training. Perhaps this can be a first step toward training corporate employees to live and work in our global world.

Acknowledgments

This book could not have been written without the support, suggestions, and editing expertise of Mary Jo Beebe. A special thanks also goes to other professionals from The Odenwald Connection: Lynn Holt, Gayle Watson, and Mary Stoddard; to my editor, Cynthia Zigmund; to Lee Schomer and Chris Fowler for their input on assessment; to Patricia Galagan for her work on executive development; to Bill Matheny for his assistance on strategy; and to Peter Beckshi and David Case for their research on design guidelines.

My sincere gratitude goes to:

The IPPA Task Force: John Eckblad, Susan Rader, BJ Chakaris, Serge Ogranovitch, Bill Shea, W. Dieter Gebhardt, Clifford Clarke, John Bing, Nessa Lowenthal, John Robinson, Steve Merman, Don Walker, Melinda Bickerstaff, and Terry Hansen.

Presenters at the 1992 ASTD pre-conference workshop in New Orleans, Louisiana: K. L. Cheah, Albert Scius, Bill Shea, Steve Ginsburgh, Bill Matheny, Richard Sands, Joyce Rogers, Barry Kozloff, Adrienne Anderson, Arash Afshar, and Don Botto.

Corporate professionals and consultants: Sharon Richards, Jeri Thornsberry, Bill Jones, Stan Horner, Roy Pendergrass, Ralph Dosher, Mary Anne Williams, Dave Dresden, Cindy Johnson, Eldon Arden, Mike Copeland, Irene DeNigris, Francoise Morissette, Sandy Hirstich, Mike Marquardt, Laura Lyons, Yves Speeckhaert, Eduardo Saleh, Rhonda Coast, Bren White, Gordon Bennett, Garry Johnson, Bob Greenleaf, and Brett Fenwick.

Current and former ASTD staff: Nancy Olson, Patricia Galagan, Mary Samsa, Edith Allen, Ramona Hadley, and Cathy Fisk.

What Is Global Training?

Everyone knows by now, the genie of international trade has long been out of the bottle.

—Anthony Carnevale
America in the New Economy

Only an ostrich could be oblivious to the fact that our business environment is not just the United States, but the world. The lines drawn between countries is blurred to the point that the terms *domestic* and *foreign* don't mean what they did 50 years ago.

TREND TO GLOBAL ENTERPRISES

The auto industry is a good example. Just a few years ago you could see a Nissan and knew it was made in Japan or felt sure the neighbor's new Jetta was made in Germany. You knew the money you spent on a Lincoln stayed here in the United States. But today, Nissans, Hondas, and Toyotas are rolling off assembly lines in the United States. Tennessee, Kentucky, and Ohio are all recipients of the Japanese automakers' desire to place their manufacturing plants in the United States. So, today, it's hard to know the nationality of a car.

And it gets even more complicated. U.S. manufacturers haven't sat idly by while other nations' companies globalized their operations. They, too, have been on the move to invest abroad. Consider that 100 percent of Jaguar and 24 percent of Mazda are now owned by Ford. Chrysler owns Lamborghini and 11 percent of Mitsubishi. General Motors is the largest American importer of cars in the United States. On the other hand, foreign automakers are busy exporting cars to their supposed countries of origin. In the process they are employing thousands of American workers at their plants in the United States.[1]

While these activities have created a climate of confusion, they have also produced incredible benefits for plant manufacturers and employees alike. The consumer, too, has benefited because the new cooperative and competitive spirit has resulted in higher productivity and much higher quality automobiles.

Global enterprise is also at work in other industries, notably in food, computers, fashion, and toys. Just imagine American Barbies and GI Joes produced in China![2]

Yes, business is definitely more global. If your company doesn't have overseas branches, then you have overseas subsidiaries. If you don't have subsidiaries, you have partners. Or you have customers. Or suppliers. The *Management Development Report* cited a National Human Resource Development (HRD) Executive Survey conducted by the American Society for Training and Development (ASTD) in 1990.[3] Forty percent of the respondents said international business is currently a significant part of their overall business, and 60 percent reported international business will increase during the next three years. One of the results of this globalization is that more and more business people are working all or part of the time in other countries or with people from other countries.

BELIEFS ABOUT GLOBAL TRAINING

Additionally, global integration has major implications for the American workforce. U.S. workers today are constantly measured against the workforces of other countries. Globalization also places new stress on workers and on management. Corporations that are highly involved in global business will find that actions taken in countries outside the United States can have unforeseen domestic impact.

Normally, training waves occur throughout corporations on the latest business emphasis. Companies eager to increase their competitiveness concentrate on areas they consider to be weaknesses that require extensive training. Consider the recent business emphasis in the United States on customer service and total quality management. An area that is gaining momentum each day as a new wave is training for a global workforce.

Why then are U.S. corporations not providing more training for their employees in this area? Would a manufacturing company design a new product and not teach its line employees how to manufacture it? Would a service company create a new service and not teach its sales staff how to sell it?

J. Stewart Black of Dartmouth's Amos Tuck School of Business Administration has surveyed expatriate U.S. executives working in Europe and Asia.[4] The fundamental reason Black found for so little global training is that U.S. companies do not believe global training is necessary. He says the assumption is that American ways and business practices are the norm, and a manager who is successful in New York or Los Angeles will also be successful in Tokyo or Brussels. Further, managers in the past have felt that foreign assignments are undesirable—a step *off* the career path.

By contrast, according to Hal Gregersen of the School of Business at Brigham Young University, companies in Japan and Britain see global experience as an integral part of the employees' management development and their promotability as well.[5] If they want to become a top-level executive, they must have global experience. So companies select them more carefully. Global corporations now incorporate global experience into a manager's career plan and provide more multicultural training for their employees worldwide.

THE NEED FOR A GLOBAL TRAINING PROCESS

While academicians and consultants indicate training is important in the United States, Black says, they often don't explain how training should be approached. So, there's nothing to help businesses or training managers understand the problem and effectively address it.

In the fall of 1990, a new training director for a midsized, high-tech company phoned with her startling discovery. "I have just learned that 63 percent of our business is conducted outside the United States, and we don't provide any training for our employees who are working internationally. What should I do? Where do we begin?" Whether American companies go global by design as part of their corporate strategy or whether they suddenly wake up to the fact that they are global in workforce and customer base, they need a process for determining what training programs are needed and who should be trained.

In assessing the available global training for employees, it was interesting to note that few corporations with whom we spoke felt they have developed a model solution. Although many companies have been providing some training for many years for employees living and working in other countries, little attention has been given to a corporatewide training strategy and process. Perhaps this situation reflects only the speed with which our world has developed into a global economy and workplace.

NEW TERMINOLOGY

In the new global environment, corporations are finding terminology important in communicating their cooperative spirit with other countries. More and more, the word *foreign* is considered inappropriate to use in describing countries other than the United States. For example, Cable News Network (CNN) President Ted Turner wants to make sure that no country feels excluded from CNN news coverage. Turner does not allow the use of the word *foreign* on his network. Instead, reporters and anchors must use the word *international* in delivering CNN's news, which now can be seen in 123 countries.

Offshore is another term that is decreasing in use since so many companies are doing business within multiple countries. The terms *global, international, multinational*, and *transnational* are sometimes used interchangeably.

DEFINITION OF GLOBAL TRAINING

So, what is global training? You will find many definitions, and most of them depend on the experiences of the person forming the answer. In San Francisco during the 1991 ASTD conference, an experienced group of corporate global training managers and consultants met to discuss current practices in global training. Several hours were spent on defining just what global training is and what it does. Selected definitions provide the necessary ingredients.

- Global training means reaching commonly defined goals with people from cultures other than one's own while treating the other's culture with deep integrity.[6]
- Global training facilitates the transfer of knowledge or skills so it can be used appropriately in the receiving environment.[7]

- Global training creates a climate in which changes in attitude, behavior, and perceptions are achieved through the sharing of knowledge and technology in a culturally appropriate way.[8]

Any training, to be effective, must be centered on the trainees—what they need to know and how to best present the knowledge and skill development to be learned. What sets global training apart is an increased focus on the background and culture of the trainees. Global training can be divided into three steps:

1. Cultivate an awareness of multicultural differences.
2. Increase specific knowledge and understanding of the trainees' culture and how their background and values influence the training process.
3. Design and present training content based on steps one and two.

The important aspects are cultural sensitivity and empathy, integrity, and sharing of knowledge and technology in the receiving environment. The difficulty lies in the true understanding of differing cultures and the framework with which people from all countries develop and share ideas.

A TIMELINE OF GLOBAL TRAINING

You may say, "But, haven't companies been training employees for overseas or offshore assignments for years? And when did global training start, and how has it evolved?"

Since the mid-twentieth century—and even earlier for some companies—corporations have established sales and manufacturing sites in various cities throughout the world. Training during these early years was generally presented in one of two ways:

1. New global employees were brought to the U.S. headquarters to learn the skills necessary to perform their work back in their countries.
2. U.S. employees were transported to the global location to teach the necessary job skills, most often through on-the-job training.

In the 1960s, most global training was done in public institutions and in universities. In a 1981 survey of 33 global companies, Michael F. Tucker and Albert Wight documented that the need for cross-cultural training was emerging.[9] George Renwick, a global consultant, made a comprehensive comparison of cross-cultural programs offered in 1973 and 1983. He found that the area of growth in this period was in the corporate sector.[10]

Stephen J. Korbrin reported in a survey published by the Institute of International Education in 1986 that global managers believed the most important factor contributing to effective management outside the United States was cross-cultural skills. This ability ranked above technical and functional skills and also over knowledge of specific industry and company information.[11]

In 1991 International Orientation Resources surveyed 50 global companies on their selection procedures for global assignments.[12] The responding corporations had a wide range in the number of years they had been sending employees to work in other countries. About 10 percent of the companies had more than 40 years' experience with global employee transfers. The majority of the companies had been sending employees for global assignments for less than 30 years. Of these companies, about 16 percent had been using expatriates for five years or less, while 48 percent had been transferring employees on global assignments for 16 to 30 years.

Many global organizations provide some orientation and training for employees who are sent to an expatriate assignment country. Vince Miller in his book, *The Guidebook for International Trainers in Business and Industry*, explains that, even in 1979, some of these training programs included language training and some orientation in the business or economic climate of the country.[13] Some instruction on travel procedures and health precautions was also mentioned. However, the most important aspect of cross-cultural and country-specific training was omitted. Here are several accounts from major corporations reflecting early global training.

Texas Instruments

Many of Texas Instruments' (TI) plant sites outside the United States were built in the 1950s and 1960s. Formalized training for employees from these various sites was accomplished through sending their engineers and technicians from other countries such as India, Italy, or Japan to American plant sites for technical training and education in how to live and work in the United States. This training not only gave these employees job knowledge but also insight into the U.S. culture. It also facilitated better current and future communications between the U.S. workforce and those in global work sites.

When TI began to send U.S. managers and trainers for "overseas" assignments, training was provided by internal employees who were from those countries or who had lived and worked there. In the mid-80s an external consulting firm that presents country-specific cultural orientation began cross-cultural seminars for TI employees and their families who were sent to plant sites outside the United States. These TI expatriates remained in that country until local employees could take over their training assignments.

TI's semiconductor division has World Training Centers in different sites around the world. The centers use instructors who provide training for that region. The best of all training courses from across the world have been consolidated and standardized into a curriculum of 15 courses.[14]

Goodyear International

Goodyear is a company with approximately $11 billion to $12 billion in sales in 1992. About 80 percent of the company's business is in tires. The global portion represents approximately 50 percent of the sales and about 60 percent of the profits. Goodyear has 50,000 associates located in 45 different countries and operates 45 different manufacturing facilities outside the United States and Canada. "We have been a global company since our first entry into Canada in 1912," says program manager Don Botto.[15] "We were conducting business in Argentina, England, and Australia in the early 1920s. So, working internationally is not new to us. We've been at it for so long. However, of all the associates we have overseas less than 200 are expatriates. That number has constantly decreased over the past 20 years. Outside the United States, we are divided into three geographic zones—Asia, Europe, and Latin America. A sales training network and a manufacturing training network have been established in each of those zones."

General Dynamics

GD has 25 sites outside the United States in 17 different countries. The largest site is in Japan and the next largest is in Taiwan. These are not GD's manufacturing sites but branches or locations for expatriate employees who consult with local nationals on the use of GD's programs. Many of these sites were opened in the 1970s. According to Bill Jones, manager of international personnel, three main groups support customers in other countries:

1. Technicians who present operational training to nationals in countries that have purchased GD's airplanes.

2. Advisors/consultants who consult with foreign coproducers on aircraft technology.

3. Designers, mostly engineers, who codevelop new aircraft with nationals from other countries outside the United States.

GD entered the global market in 1975 and has continued to expand its overseas operations to the current level. GD began using external consultants in 1981 to train its U.S. employees who were selected for assignments at its international locations. The employees, their spouses, and children were given training in the culture and value systems of the customers in their assigned countries. Because of this training and a thorough screening system through which GD chose long-term employees who were committed to the company and their assignments, expatriates' failure rates have been extremely low. Some employees who were assigned for a short term requested a longer term assignment or even two or three consecutive assignments at global sites. Approximately 200 employees are in deployment or reentry during the course of a year, and the company has an estimated 350 expatriates at global locations.

Several years after establishing the cultural training for expatriates, GD personnel realized that the culture shock of coming back to the United States with the changes in lifestyle and workplace needed to be addressed. They began repatriation training for expatriates who were reassigned to U.S. positions. Bill Jones and his staff, along with the external consultants who provide these cross-cultural programs, have one of the most successful track records of any U.S. corporation in the training of expatriates and their families.[16]

AT&T

Globalization is a top strategy for AT&T. Geraldine M. Thornsberry, district manager of international education and training in the International Operations Division, states that her team supports three primary work groups that are located outside the United States:

1. Managers who work directly with PTT correspondents.

2. Sales support personnel.

3. Administrative support staff.

These groups, both expatriates and country nationals, are provided technical, cross-cultural, sales skills, and managerial and advanced business training for the country in which AT&T is located.[17]

AT&T International Operations Division maintains offices in 42 cities throughout the world. As you can imagine, locations in Mexico City, Vancouver, British Columbia, Paris, New Delhi, Hong Kong, Tokyo, and Beijing—to name a few—offer unique challenges and opportunities for employee education.

AT&T's education programs raise awareness of cultural differences and the need for negotiation skills plus the importance of teamwork. Training is primarily delivered in English but can be supplemented by native speakers or tutors when necessary. Trainers come from varied backgrounds within the company and from numerous locations across the globe depending on the type of training needed.

3M

3M began establishing a global presence in the late 1940s and currently has 52 subsidiaries around the world. In 1981, Eldon Arden, manager of management development, set up a staff development training program to help local employees in other countries improve their competencies and skills.[18] Since 3M is highly decentralized, training was presented through the 50 different businesses. During the past three years, 3M has begun multicultural training for employees. Cindy Johnson, manager of supervisory and individual development programs, is responsible for 400 courses for more than 20,000 employees in the United States. For example, U.S. employees are trained in a program on working with the Japanese. Similarly, 3M employees at the Somotoma, Japan, site take part in a program that helps them work with Americans. This training is designed on two levels, beginning and intermediate, and consists of two days each. The program is for supervisors and managers and is presented by external consultants.

In 1990, "The Art of Crossing Cultures," a training program on cultural awareness, was designed for all 3M employees. Currently, this course is offered twice a year. Also, a Language Society offers one-on-one tutoring and classes during the lunch hour on French, Spanish, and other languages for company employees from all levels.

"An exciting new training project we are working on is our Leadership Continuum program," states Johnson.[19] The program will build on a continuum from employee level to supervisory, management, and executive levels. A worldwide task force is in place to identify the competencies needed at all levels, determine what training is needed for specific behaviors, and set training priorities and strategy. This information will then be tested in the different geographic areas of Asia, Africa, Latin America, Europe, and the United States. The feedback from employees in 40 different countries will be collected, and a core of courses with cultural variances will be developed from this research. The company hopes to roll out several levels of courses the first year. It also plans cross-functional assignments through electronic mail, as well as in-group sessions to provide a broader perspective for 3M global teams.

In the near future 3M hopes to incorporate modules of global training into all supervisory courses. Country-specific training will also be provided as needed. Johnson believes training employees in cultural differences can impact the bottom line and can save them from costly mistakes. "As these programs are developed, training managers should involve employees in other countries in the analysis and design, asking them about what experience and education they need, to get buy in and global support for the training. It's exciting," Johnson continues, "to watch as employees experience the training and begin to think globally and become more globally competitive. Training can add lots of value to the success of a global corporation."

Baxter International

"For the past six years, Baxter, a health care corporation, has provided multicultural training for employees and spouses moving to an assignment outside the United States," says Dave Dresden, director of international assignments.[20] "This training addresses the specific needs of each employee. Some expatriates have had no international experience, and others have traveled extensively outside the United States and even lived in other parts of the world. So the cultural training should fit the employee's experience and knowledge of that country," Dresden states.

Cross-cultural training is provided by external consultants. Eighty employees currently are on assignment outside their base country. Of this group, 60 are from the United States, 25 are "inpatriates"—employees from other countries who are on assignment at the U.S. corporate headquarters, and 10 are transfers from one country to another. The average length of an individual assignment is for two and one-half to three years.

Dresden advises, "Before you begin a multicultural training program, be sure you understand the needs of those who will be trained. You should do a thorough needs assessment and develop the training around those needs. Some managers have worked in similar cultures and have international savvy, and you do not want to place them at the same basic level as a manager who has had no cross-cultural experience." Although the focus at Baxter has been on expatriate or impatriate training, it has begun a pilot program for employees who travel to other countries on business for the company. In the future, Baxter hopes to provide multicultural training for more employees who interact with people in other countries.

CURRENT TRENDS AND PRACTICES

A breakdown in multicultural communication usually occurs when the individuals involved do not understand the differences between their cultures. Subconsciously, members of each culture group assume that all people around the world share their perceptions and beliefs. Most of us have tunnel vision and are so locked into our own culture that we do not see the subtle differences in other cultures.

To combat this attitude and train employees in cultural awareness, international training departments began appearing on corporate organizational charts. These departments were given the task of providing training for company employees living and working in other countries. Today, separate international departments are disappearing. The integration of global training into other training programs and areas is a current trend. Global issues are incorporated into product development, and the marketing and sales departments address how to market and sell these products globally. Cultural awareness training is often a module of other courses such as management training.

Although global training is still in its infancy stage, many corporations are recognizing that training on how to conduct business outside the United States can effectively increase productivity and profits. Employees who understand the nuances of other cultures and value systems can communicate more clearly and build meaningful business relationships with peers, customers, and suppliers internationally. The message is urgent for human resource professionals in today's global workplace: **Global training must lead the way**. The sharing of information about global training strategy and design between training managers can help corporations become more effective global competitors.

Chapter One

Assessing Global Training Needs

The strategy, culture, and people of an organization must all go global together.

Stephen H. Rhinesmith
"An Agenda for Globalization"
Training & Development, February 1991

A s corporations become more global, the issues of training American employees to work in other countries, manage employees in those countries, and deal with customers internationally becomes more imperative. Companies that currently provide some cross-cultural training realize they should have a more systematic approach. So, assessing all employees to determine who needs global training and what training should be provided is essential in designing an effective multicultural training program.

Taking American ideas into other countries without taking cultural difference into consideration is generally detrimental in global management. Most often what worked in the United States does not work in other countries. Corporations must train their employees to expand their horizons beyond domestic issues to think and work from a global perspective. The fact that many Americans believe that they have nothing to learn from other countries is also a major barrier.

MOVING FROM DOMESTIC TO GLOBAL

Going global is a complex process, but it's not limited to big, established companies. As soon as a corporation moves outside its home base, to sell, operate, or invest in any way in other countries, it could be on its way to being global. Since World War II, corporations have progressed from domestic operations to more global strategies. Global consultant and professor Nancy Adler describes the globalization process as a four-phase evolution that takes a company from domestic, to international, to multinational, and finally, to global operations.[1] She characterizes these four stages by looking at the company's competitive strategy, the extent to which it shares technology, its market, and its organizational structure. One method that Adler has used to examine the evolution of global firms is through its products and services. What follows is a pattern for thinking about international human resource management and international strategy. Figure 1–1 outlines a four-phase evolution from a domestic company to a global one.[2]

Phase I—Domestic Phase. Companies in Phase I operate on domestic terms and focus on developing a product or service based on state-of-the-art technology. Viewing the United States as a large market in which they can prosper, Phase I companies have traditionally been highly successful and have not had to look outside the borders of the United States for additional markets. With the increase of diversity within domestic companies, however, training is now addressing the need for cultural awareness and multicultural training within domestic firms. Corporations that provide this training realize it increases communication and effectiveness in self-directed work teams.

Phase II—International Phase. As additional domestic companies are established, competition increases. Corporations are then forced to search for new markets or lose market share. Adler explains that a common response is to expand worldwide, first by exporting to markets outside the United States. Later in this expansion, firms develop manufacturing and production sites in other countries to serve the largest of their markets. Often, U.S. companies initially export to their closest neighbors, Mexico or Canada, or into another English-speaking country such as Great Britain. Usually in such companies, international human resource development activities focus only on the small group of expatriate managers involved directly in foreign operations. Training for these expatriates and their families is single-country focused and culturally specific. Structurally, the company often forms a single international division for its foreign operations.

FIGURE 1–1
International Corporate Evolution

	PHASE I	PHASE II	PHASE III	PHASE IV
	Domestic	**International**	**Multinational**	**Global**
Competitive strategy	Domestic	Multidomestic	Multinational	Global
Importance of world business	Marginal	Important	Extremely important	Dominant
Primary orientation	Product or service	Market	Price	Strategy
Product/ service	New, unique	More standardized	Completely standardized (commodity)	Mass-customized
	Product engineering emphasized	Process engineering emphasized	Engineering not emphasized	Product and process engineering
Technology	Proprietary	Shared	Widely shared	Instantly and extensively shared
Research and development/sales	High (10%–14%)	Decreasing	Very low	High
Profit margin	High	Decreasing	Very low	High
Competitors	None	Few	Many	Significant (few or many)
Market	Small, domestic	Large, multidomestic	Larger, multinational	Largest, global
Production location	Domestic	Domestic and primary markets	Multinational, least cost	Global, least cost
Exports	None	Growing, high potential	Large and saturated	Imports and exports
Structure	Functional divisions	Functional with international division	Multinational lines of business	Global alliance heteroarchy
	Centralized	Decentralized	Centralized	Centralized and decentralized

Unfortunately, international managers in this phase are often viewed as out of the corporate mainstream and slightly out-of-date.

Phase III—Multinational Phase. Companies in Phase III focus on least-cost production with sourcing, manufacturing, and marketing worldwide. Selected local managers from subsidiaries outside the United States are sometimes sent on inpatriate assignments to the U.S. company headquarters. Structurally, multinational corporations often reorganize into global lines of business. Cultural differences then begin to move into the organizational culture itself. The emergence of cross-cultural dynamics becomes a critical aspect of organizational functioning for the multicultural company.

Phase IV—Global Phase. The company in this phase is truly global and operates worldwide. Cross-cultural interaction is everywhere, both in the corporation and with customers and clients. Multiculturalism dominates the organization's culture. Fluid strategic alliances now define the organization's form and structure. Global thinking and global competencies become critical for survival and success. In these corporations global human resource strategies are being developed together with training in multicultural management.

As firms move through the four phases, the level of cross-cultural interface moves up the organization from the individual contributor into management and on into the executive arena. Phase I companies rarely send managers abroad and depend on diversity training for their multicultural domestic workforce. In Phase II, companies' cultural differences strongly affect relationships with potential buyers and international employees, so these firms frequently send their better, more senior managers abroad. By Phase IV, companies send their fast-track junior managers and their most senior executives on expatriate assignments. Skill at multicultural management takes on increasing importance with each phase. This progression of culture from lack of importance to criticality, underlies and influences the company's human resource management and training strategies.[3] (See Figure 1–2: Corporate Cross-Cultural Evolution.)

Directors of corporate training must first determine which classification on the continuum fits their company's operations. This determination can be made from research inside the corporation. Corporate mission and strategy statements, annual reports, corporate brochures, marketing reports, yearly sales figures, policies and procedures manuals, and other such documents provide important data for this determination. If the top training manager is not on the executive decision-making team, additional information can come

FIGURE 1–2
Corporate Cross-Cultural Evolution

	PHASE I	PHASE II	PHASE III	PHASE IV
	Domestic	International	Multinational	Global
Primary orientation	Product/ service	Market	Price	Strategy
Strategy	Domestic	Multidomestic	Multinational	Global
Perspective	Ethnocentric	Polycentric or regiocentric	Multinational	Global/ multicentric
Cultural sensitivity	Unimportant	Very important	Somewhat important	Critically important
With whom	No one	Clients	Employees	Employees and clients
Level	No one	Workers and clients	Managers	Executives
Strategic assumption	"One-way" or "One-best-way"	"Many-best-ways" equifinality	"One-least cost-way"	"Many-best-ways" simultaneously

through interviews or correspondence with executives to assess current practices and future strategic directions.

A truly domestic corporation assesses domestic suppliers, produces services and/or products domestically, and markets and sells only to local country customers. However, because of the trends of global movement and immigration, U. S. demographics reveal an increasingly diverse workforce. Therefore, multicultural training for the domestic corporation entails addressing diversity issues within the company's workforce. Determining the nationalities and cultures of domestic employees, the number of employees representing each culture, their language capabilities or restrictions, their job requirements, and how specific cultures affect teamwork become important criteria for training strategy and design.

Domestic companies in today's environment can no longer disregard global factors that affect their businesses. These factors include domestic markets and profits, the effects of competition from global companies, economic conditions in other countries, the influx of capital from other countries, and joint ventures partnering U.S. firms with companies outside its borders.

In *A Manager's Guide to Globalization*, Stephen H. Rhinesmith identifies a new form of domestic company that is now part of the global economy.[4]

Domestic corporations, especially American retail stores such as K-Mart and Bloomingdale's, now source globally for production and sales. They no longer manufacture only in the United States for their growing global market. Corporations have traditionally gone outside the United States to take advantage of lower prices in raw materials and wages. However, these companies view themselves as purely domestic enterprises, using U.S. manufacturing sites to produce products for their domestic markets although they may go to Japan for financing, India for engineers, or Germany for technology. These global domestic firms are usually created and run by managers and top-level executives who have developed a global view but since these corporations enjoy profits in their American market, they often have no incentives to market worldwide.

Planning a training program for the global domestic company and the international corporation—the company that has an international division that works separately from the main domestic operations—must include more than diversity training. These organizations must at least provide courses on cultural awareness, cross-cultural skills, and executive development on global conditions. An assessment of which employees communicate and work with suppliers, customers, and employees in identified countries and cultures will help drive the decision on who to train and what knowledge and level of skills they need.

When a U.S. corporation moves on the continuum to multinational status, it is, in essence, establishing domestic arms in other countries. These international sales offices or plant sites are organized like their domestic operations and are extensions of the corporation in other parts of the world. Such companies are committed to working in many countries and often pride themselves in turning over to local employees the management of their operations outside the U.S. borders. An objective of this type of organization is to be viewed as a domestic corporation with multiple sites around the world. These companies hope that local regulatory authorities will look at the local entity as a national unit. Thus, the firm gains a domestic competitive advantage by globally sourced resources, competencies, and technology.

While some training of managers for international assignments occurs in the international company category, expatriate training for the multinational organization becomes a necessity. Because of the large number of local employees working at global sites, an assessment, such as the one suggested later in this chapter, should extend to employees worldwide. This type of survey becomes more difficult as language and communication factors are built into the process. However, without adequate information obtained through surveying the organization's population, training will be a shotgun approach—haphazard and based on supposition rather than true needs.

Instead of delegating international business to a separate international department or setting up replicas of domestic operations outside the United States, the global corporation shares resources worldwide to get access to the best market with the highest quality product at the lowest cost. Rhinesmith cites several firms who have successfully moved into the global arena:

> Global organizations like IBM, GE, McDonald's, Ford, Shell, Philips, Sony, NCR, and Unilever have shed their national identity, are highly adaptive to changes in the environment, and are extremely sensitive to all global trends that may affect the future. This is a very different and very sophisticated form of organization, as well as business strategy. It requires a completely different mindset and very adaptable managers and corporate cultures.[5]

Training for the global organization must provide a framework for changing the mindset of the executives, managers, and employees to focus on globalization. No longer can they think strategically or operationally from a domestic frame of reference. They must develop a global mindset, which means unlearning old methods and opening up to a new way of thinking and working globally. The Band-Aid approach now used by most corporations may offer temporary relief but will not move the corporation forward effectively to meet its desired goals. As Adler points out, Phase IV managers must face the fact that the salient question is not *if* there is cultural diversity, but rather *how* to manage it.[6] Following an assessment process, a comprehensive training strategy can be designed and implemented.

Some considerations for assessing global needs are:

- Identifying employees who work in cross-cultural situations.
- Determining who is to be trained and how.
- Identifying topic areas that are currently not being covered.
- Starting with the end result of training—the objective.

WHO TO TRAIN, HOW MUCH TO TRAIN

Corporate globalization also increases the need for effective multicultural communication as it multiplies the number of contacts between U.S. employees of all levels and peers, partners, and suppliers in other countries. These contacts are often between individuals at varied levels of responsibility and include correspondence, phone, and fax communication and meetings with visitors from various countries. As Gary M. Wederspahn of Moran, Stahl & Boyer's International Division says, "Conflicting cultural values regarding hospitality, politeness, and respect increase the risk of creating misunderstanding, friction, and disappointment on both sides. These problems damage the image of the company, lower the morale of employees, and may irritate important global customers or partners."[7]

Training money is often limited, and global training can be expensive. So how do you choose who to train and what training to give them? If technicians are going to another country to install equipment in a short period of time, it may be too costly and time intensive to provide cross-cultural training.[8] But for managers and employees on long-term global assignment, training becomes more important. For this reason, many corporations are training their employees for communicating, living, and working outside the United States. To effectively meet global training needs, training managers must know what training is necessary and who should be trained. However, as is true with any new training area, needs assessment methodology for global training is still in the developmental stages. The following needs assessment survey discussion is one a company could use to identify the extent and character of its multicultural work: the contacts made with people in other countries, the role of these contacts, the amount of time spent, type of contacts, and skills the employees think are critical for quality communication. A survey of this type can help a corporation get a good overview of employees' involvement in multicultural business relations. It helps establish the foundation for more thorough individual interviews and focus groups that can further identify needs.

To collect data in an assessment of the employees of the global corporation, special attention should be given to the following aspects:[9]

I. Process

    A. A clear link should be made to tie the survey results data to corporate strategic and annual operating plans and budgets.

    B. Total customization of the survey is required in terms of design, output requirements, format, data processing specifications, communication of results, and user applications. This set of considerations is also a function of the budget constraints, physical aspects of the operating countries, workforce size, geography, etc.

    C. The company's position on the continuum from domestic to global and the speed with which the company is moving into the global marketplace heavily influence the requirements of the survey.

    D. The collection of the data should be timed in two cycles:

1. The workforce assessment. This survey for all employees should be conducted on an 18-month cycle for the core questionnaire on operational benchmarks of the company and its workforce.

2. The training data report. This collection of data from the workforce assessment should be conducted every 36 months to update total human resource and global training data bases, demographics, and related business plans.

II. Quantitatively based methods

To be effective, the assessment should be aimed at full company employment tabulation and not just a sampling. The suggested survey methods are:

A. Customized paper and pencil questionnaire.

B. Customized electronic mail questionnaire (remote 24 hours).

C. Customized tele-poll (remote dial-in/24 hours).

III. Applications

The information collected can be used as the basis for designing and presenting training for:

A. Americans who work in other countries as expatriates.

B. Americans managing multicultural and global employees.

C. Managers dealing with global customers.

D. *Other country* nationals to work in the United States.

IV. Job aspects

The information requested varies according to the specific corporation. So the examples provided are guidelines that can be used to develop a company-focused questionnaire. The assessment data should cover certain job aspects, such as:

A. Cultural values and behaviors—from symbols to actions.

1. Hospitality.

2. Politeness and respect behaviors.

3. Business protocols.

4. Time (uses of time).

B. Language.

C. Communications.

1. Mediums: print, face-to-face, telephone, video.

2. Mode: most favored versus most effective.

3. Frequency.

D. Technical skills required for the job and assignments.

E. Physical living and working requirements.

    1. Climate/attire.

    2. Legal.

    3. Security.

    4. Financial.

    5. Medical.

    6. Schools.

    7. Social.

    8. Religious.

    9. Political.

    10. Job duties/roles/business contacts.

The global training manager must secure the highest level of commitment from corporate executives not just to collect the data, but also to use the information for training strategy and implementation. Only when the collective data is actually used as a basis for training will the time, effort, and money spent on the assessment be worthwhile. Let's now look at some guidelines for a corporate workforce assessment.[10]

A SAMPLE INTERCULTURAL RELATIONS SURVEY FOR U.S. PERSONNEL

Purpose

As a company becomes more global in scope, what happens globally influences it as never before. Let's look at one firm's organizational structure, management systems, employee language requirements, and technical and interpersonal skills required to successfully compete in today's global marketplace. Let's assess the company's intercultural business relationships with employees, affiliated companies, customers, and suppliers in overseas locations. Your responses will help to analyze the nature and extent of the intercultural contacts and the training necessary to facilitate the communications. We are seeking information in three major areas:

A. The nature of the overseas contact you maintain.

    1. Overseas contacts with company employees who are nationals.

2. Overseas contacts with nationals who are suppliers, distributors, and/or manufacturers.

3. Overseas contacts with nationals who are customers.

B. The amount of time spent on various types of contacts. Please also assess the amount of communication occurring by phone, electronic mail, fax, telex, and face-to-face.

C. The skills you think are essential to establish and maintain high-quality intercultural communication.

1. Overseas contacts with company employees who are nationals.
   Instructions:

   - On the following matrix, list the home countries of the company employee nationals you contact on a regular basis.

   - List the key job functions (i.e., reporting, ordering, performance issues, equipment repair, etc.) you discuss regularly with company employee nationals.

   - Record, under the appropriate country, the approximate number of hours per month you spend in the intercultural contacts.

Job functions discussed	Countries contacted regularly						
	#1	#2	#3	#4	#5	#6	#7
1.							
2.							
3.							
4.							
5.							
6.							
7.							
8.							
9.							
10.							

Typical problems that impede the effectiveness of these contacts are: _____

2. Overseas contacts with nationals who are suppliers, distributors, and/or manufacturers.
   Instructions:

   - On the following matrix, list the home countries of the suppliers, distributors, and/or manufacturers you contact on a regular basis.
   - Designate the type of person you contact (e.g., supplier, distributor, manufacturer).
   - List the key job functions (e.g., reporting, ordering, performance issues, equipment repair, etc.) you discuss regularly with these nationals.
   - Record, under the appropriate country, the approximate number of hours per month you spend in the intercultural contacts.

Person—job function	Countries contacted regularly						
	#1	#2	#3	#4	#5	#6	#7
1.							
2.							
3.							
4.							
5.							
6.							
7.							
8.							
9.							
10.							

Typical problems that impede the effectiveness of these contacts are: _____

_____

3. Overseas contacts with nationals who are customers.
   Instructions:

   - On the following matrix, list the home countries of the customers you contact on a regular basis.
   - Designate the name of the customer and/or company.

- List the key job functions (e.g., reporting, ordering, performance issues, equipment repair, etc.) you discuss with these nationals regularly.
- Record, under the appropriate country, the approximate number of hours per month you spend in the intercultural contacts.

Person—job function	Countries contacted regularly						
	#1	#2	#3	#4	#5	#6	#7
1.							
2.							
3.							
4.							
5.							
6.							
7.							
8.							
9.							
10.							

Typical problems that impede the effectiveness of these contacts are: _____

_____

B. Time spent in various types of contacts.

Please indicate the approximate percentage of time you spend in each type of intercultural communication. Your estimates should total 100%.

_____ Telephone
_____ Written (including electronic mail and fax)
_____ Face-to-face
100% Total

What do you think *should* be the distribution of time spent in each type of contact?

_____ Telephone
_____ Written (including electronic mail and fax)
_____ Face-to-face
100% Total

Do you feel you maintain your intercultural contacts effectively? If not, what keeps you from maintaining them the way you would recommend?

_____

_____

_____

C. Intercultural communication skills

Please rate each of the following intercultural skills with regard to "importance to job" and "level of competence." Add any additional skills you believe are important. Under "importance to job," indicate how essential you think the skill is to maintain the intercultural communications in your job. (Use a "1" to represent "very essential," a "2" to represent "good to be able to do, but not essential," and a "3" to represent "not needed.") Under "level of competence," indicate whether you think you would benefit from training in the skill. (Use "1" to represent "would benefit from training" and "2" to represent "training not beneficial.")

Communication skills	Importance to job	Level of competence
1. Speak plain, simple English.		
2. Paraphrase the speaker's words.		
3. Demonstrate acceptance of another's words or actions even though you may disagree or disapprove of his or her actions.		
4. Express appreciation.		
5. Give instructions without patronizing.		
6. Write clear memos, proposals, and reports.		
7. Express disagreement in a constructive way.		
8._____		
9._____		
10._____		

D. Languages

What level of language knowledge do you require to do your job effectively?

Please check the appropriate answer.

_____ Conversation: typical greetings and a few social phrases.

_____ Verbal fluency.
_____ Written fluency.

Languages	Check the languages in which you are fluent			Check the ones you need to learn to be more effective in your job		
	Conversation	Verbal	Written	Conversation	Verbal	Written
English						
German						
French						
Spanish						
Japanese						
Italian						
Arabic						
Other						

E. Cultural background

Check the items that you think are essential to know about a national's culture in order to establish and maintain an effective business relationship with that person.

___ History

___ Government structure

___ Political realities

___ Social taboos

___ Labor laws

___ Taxation policies

___ Religion and religious practices

___ Educational systems

___ Philosophy and logic of the ethical systems

___ Currency

___ Values

___ Socially acceptable behaviors

___ Family customs

___ Marriage customs

___ Foods and diet

___ Traffic regulations

___ Typical recreational activities

___ Laws and regulations related to work

CORPORATE SURVEY DATA

After the surveys are completed and returned, the data from the corporation's employee intercultural survey is collected and tabulated. This information provides a view of the global activities of company employees and becomes the basis to determine what training is needed. The collective data should answer such questions as:

- How many company employees work in countries outside the United States? In which countries? What job functions do they perform?
- How many employees travel to other countries as part of their job responsibilities? How many times per year? How long do they remain there?
- How many U.S. employees correspond with employees in other countries? Talk by phone with employees in other countries? Which countries? How many employees in each country? How often?
- How many U.S. employees talk/correspond/work with customers in other countries? Which countries? How many customers in each country? How often?
- How many U.S. employees talk/correspond/work with suppliers in other countries? Which countries? How many suppliers in each country? How often?
- How many employees speak a language other than English? How many are fluent in another language? Which language(s)?

After these questions are answered, the corporation's top-level executives can provide additional data on the corporate business strategy and future directions. Questions like the following are important for management to consider:

- At the present time, which country is targeted as the main focus of your company's business?
- What countries buy or use your company's products and/or services?
- Do you plan to expand to other countries? Which one(s)?
- In which countries are you partnering with other companies or groups?
- How do customers view your company? How can you improve?
- Where are there performance problems? Where do you need to improve your skills?
- How can you better prepare people for assignments? How much time and money should you invest in this effort?

This cumulative employee and company survey data, information from individual interviews and focus groups can then become a basis for driving the training program for the entire corporation. Training strategy and decisions can be based on what multicultural skills are needed by specific employees rather than on assumptions that a particular global training course sounds interesting and might meet company needs.

When corporations decide to assess employee multicultural needs, they should consider an efficient method of obtaining survey information. A team at AT&T found that electronic mail is an effective way of obtaining responses to an employee questionnaire. According to Lorraine Parker of AT&T's International Operations Division, its Process Quality Management and Improvement team was given the responsibility of researching the company's expatriation and repatriation processes.[11] The employees surveyed were working abroad in many different countries and time zones. Electronic mail provided a fast and easy-to-use format that was not hampered by various time zones. The team also felt that the 68 percent response rate was higher because of their use of the electronic delivery system.

For corporations to succeed in any phase in their evolution from domestic business to global operations, a thorough understanding of multicultural training needs must be gained. Needs assessment is critical for this understanding. The methods mentioned in this chapter for obtaining information will help the organization attain a complete and balanced view upon which to base a training strategy.

Chapter Two

Assisting Management to Think Globally

To say that the world is getting smaller is a cliché.
To say that ultimately the only effective way to deal with it
is through the development of intercultural skills is
profound and revolutionary.

—David S. Hoopes
Global Guide to International Business

Most business leaders in the United States have been focused on the domestic market for so long that it is difficult to develop the knowledge, skills, cultural sensitivity, and experience to win in global markets. Changing from a domestic focus to a global mindset takes a major shift in attitude and a willingness to allocate time and money for skill development. "As a consequence, one of the transnational manager's primary skills is to exercise discretion in choosing when to be locally responsive and when to emphasize global integration," states Nancy Adler.[1]

Moreover, the integration required in global firms is based on "cultural synergy—on combining the many cultures into a unique organizational culture—rather than on simply integrating foreigners into the dominant culture of the headquarters' nationality (as was the norm in prior phases)," Adler continues. The additional new skills managers require to be effective in their less hierarchical, networked firms are:

- The ability to work with people of other cultures as equals.
- The ability to learn in order to continually enhance organizational capability.

Global managers must learn how to collaborate with partners worldwide, gain as much knowledge as possible from each interaction, and transmit that knowledge quickly and effectively throughout their worldwide operations network. This expertise requires managers who have both the desire to learn and the skills to quickly and continuously learn from the culturally diverse global workforce.

To follow a new global paradigm, managers must constantly deal with fear and uncertainty. As Gareth Morgan declares in *Riding the Waves of Change: Developing Managerial Competencies for a Turbulent World,* "Numerous technological, social, and information revolutions are combining to create a degree of flux that often challenges the fundamental assumptions on which organizations and their managers have learned to operate."[2] In *Managing as a Performing Art*, Peter Vaill agrees as he calls today's uncertainty and turbulence *permanent white water.*[3] Vaill describes the challenges facing global managers in his discussion of white-water rafting. "They're led to believe that they should be pretty much able to go where they want, when they want, using means that are under their controls.... But it has been my experience that they never get out of the rapids!"

White-water rafting is perhaps the best analogy global managers can use to think of their responsibilities. Stephen H. Rhinesmith points out that the global manager's world requires constant adaptation to its complexity.[4] It also involves managing culturally diverse teams. In today's complex world, things often seem out of control. However, learning to *go with the flow* is a fundamental part of global management. Global executives and managers must learn to think globally and develop a global mindset. "Any global manager who is afraid to occasionally let go will be doomed to be left behind, concentrating on control, while the world—and opportunities—flow away," Rhinesmith explains.

In a forward-looking article, "Executive Development in a Changing World," Editor Patricia A. Galagan interviewed members of the American Society for Training and Development's (ASTD's) board of governors and corporate executives on this important topic. The main text of that article is reprinted over the next 11 pages as it presents special insight on helping managers to think globally.[5]

What will it mean to be an executive in a world that is rushing to become a single economy? What will it take to lead a corporation in a global marketplace where economic considerations are likely to be more important than political ones? What skills, still unlearned, and what kind of mindset, still undeveloped, will executives have to master in order to survive?

According to experts, most executives have a lot to learn to be effective. For starters, most executives must begin to see their companies in a global context, even if they don't operate outside national boundaries. Then they will have to bring everyone in their company to the same vision, even in the face of uncertainty. Along the way, executives will have to know themselves, learn at hyperspeed, and be the teachers-in-chief of their organizations.

Opinion varies greatly about what kind of development executives need most. Posing the question "What are the key issues facing executives today?" produced 79 different answers from 19 executive developers surveyed by ASTD's board of governors.

"The greatest barrier facing the executives whom I see is their lack of clear perception of where they're going," says Mathew Juechter, who works routinely with top executives. "One of their main tasks is to energize organizations to have the will to act, and to do this they need to know how and why an organization's structure prevents action."

Consultant Geary Rummler believes that tomorrow's executives "need to think and operate globally and be able to drive that through the organization." In the opinion of Nancy Adler, professor of management at McGill University, they need "to develop the skills for global competitiveness." The executive of the nineties will be someone who "makes good decisions in the face of rapidly changing variables," says Paul Cimmerer, manager of HRD at Cray Research.

Many people who work with executives believe they take too little interest in their own development. As business goes global, what should executives and their developers be learning? For guidance, the American Society for Training and Development, through its board of governors, sought the best ideas of some prominent executive developers. A special supplement to the *Training & Development Journal* reported on their ideas and recommendations.

Going Global in the Nineties

Global, the buzzword, will soon be reality. What is not so clear is its precise meaning. What's intended by this popular new business term?

Global is the way the world is headed at breakneck speed, say *Megatrends 2000* authors John Naisbitt and Patricia Aburdene. Global is where we already are, according to Stephen H. Rhinesmith, a consultant who works extensively in the Soviet Union.

Even though global is an idea still under development, it is already changing some people's perceptions of doing business. As long as domestic markets were strong and relatively independent of foreign competition, American companies and their executives could get along with a low-grade awareness of what was going on in the rest of the world. When American managers travelled offshore, they came back with anecdotal evidence that culture mattered when doing business abroad, but for the most part they didn't change the way their companies did business in other countires. It's not that they didn't learn from their experiences and the cautionary tales of other travellers. Americans travelling abroad on business learned not to use the wrong (left) hand in India, ask the wrong (personal) questions in the Middle East, or make the wrong (direct) eye contact in Japan.

Even after many American companies became multinationals, a foreign assignment was not meant to enrich corporate understanding of doing business in a broader context. The men (yes, it was almost always men) who were sent abroad for long assignments came home a little too foreign for Illinois or wherever headquarters happened to be. They came back with plenty of cultural sensitivity and no career prospects. Quickly they learned that they were on the fast track to oblivion.

Today, however, it is harder to define the nationality of a company by its location or its ownership or its workers. As economist Robert Reich writes in "Who is Us?" (*Harvard Business Review*, January-February 1990), it's time to "rethink our ideas of national competitiveness based solely on ownership." A company might have American directors and shareholders, but mostly non-American employees doing research and development, product design, and manufacturing outside the United States. Conversely, a foreign-owned company might do most of its manufacturing in the United States and export its product—made in America by Americans—to the Far East.

Multinational identity is not new for American companies, but employing large percentages of foreigners is new. At IBM, for instance, 40 percent of the worldwide workforce is not American.

Call It Global

As it stands now, *global* is the popular term for companies that have fully integrated operations—product design, process design, manufacturing, and vendor management—in many parts of the world. For example, Honda, the Japanese carmaker, has a fully integrated operation in the United States for producing the Honda Accord Coupe. The car was designed and is produced only in the United States and is mainly sold in the United States. Ford Motor Company has a similar operation in Europe.

At the point where global strategy and human resource management intersect, there is a big void in knowledge and practice, says Adler. But as her research shows, there is a new developmental path for executives in global companies, and it is via the once-deadly expatriate assignment. "Being sent abroad in a company's domestic phase can mean you're definitely not on the fast track. While in today's later stages, an expatriate assignment is a route to the top."

Global Success Factors:
What the Experts Say

To be a successful executive in a global world is going to take some special knowledge and skills, much of it new and some of it paradoxical. As Badi Foster, president of the Aetna Institute for Corporate Education, points out, "There is a lot of intellectual work ahead for executives."

One tough challenge for executives is to learn to think differently than in the past. In many cases this means changing a mindset that the executive believes got him or her to the top. Michael Doyle, an international consultant on large-scale organizational change, says, "We must help move senior executives toward breakthrough thinking." Merlin Davidson, director of human resources, planning, and development for Bethlehem Steel, says "One of our biggest issues is getting executives to think globally." But Adler disagrees. "It's time for executives to move beyond an awareness of the urgency of global competitiveness and begin to develop skills for success in the global arena."

Joseph DiStefano, who has been teaching cross-cultural awareness for 20 years at the University of Western Ontario School of Business Administration, also thinks executives must push themselves into new intellectual territory. "To think and behave competently on a global basis, executives have to get beyond the ability to work internationally. It's not enough anymore."

Another framework to break, says DiStefano, is the American focus on the individual. "It isn't just executives who will carry all that weight of learning and relearning. Everyone in the organization has to reconceptualize."

Effectiveness Based on Fit

"A first step is knowing where you are," says DiStefano. "It's important to be able to type your organization. Is it global or just getting there?" DiStefano offers these guidelines for integrating global awareness into a company's total strategy: redefine the structure, the key tasks for success, and the kinds of people needed to implement the strategy in light of the new global imperatives; check that the organizational design elements reinforce each other and do not contradict each other; redesign the major administrative systems—recruiting, selection, training and development, information, performance management, and rewards—to serve the new global needs of the company; check that these systems too are congruent with the organization, key tasks, and people as redefined to implement a global strategy.

For DiStefano the big picture of how business operates must include an appreciation for the paradox of thinking globally and acting locally. "Business strategies may become more standardized in a company, yet there will be local variations. Executives will have to get their minds around the contradiction between standardized strategies and different implementation in different regions of the world."

The adage to know thyself organizationally is reinforced by Juechter, whose consulting practice focuses primarily on executive development and strategic planning. "The work that I find most challenging has to do with executives' understanding of organizational life cycles. I don't think there's a clear view among executives of when to transition and when to transform. Those are fundamentally different and they require different leadership techniques. I don't think there's sufficient clarity around that difference, especially when there's a need to anticipate rather than react to changes generated by life cycle issues.

"I'm very concerned when I see executives focused primarily on internal, organizational issues rather than developing a larger sense of how businesses stay successful over time," says Juechter.

"Global is a condition in which all boundaries are broken down," says Rhinesmith. "The nineties are a time to rethink not just boundaries of place, but structural and functional boundaries within the organization. Working with global companies has shown me that one of their biggest challenges is to get managers and executives to change their frames of reference."

What to Teach

"In executive programs," says Rhinesmith, "we have to deliver new types of information about the world, and in my view, the profession still needs to define the critical elements of this information—the overall social, political, economic, and cultural issues. How do you define global in a way that makes sense to an executive? I define a global company as one that is delivering high-quality products at the lowest price to the best possible markets anywhere in the world. And it uses global sourcing of capital, technology, facilities, human resources, and raw materials in ways that are constantly changing. The ability to look at all these areas in a new way is a starting point for distinguishing between global and multinational managers.

"Executives are already good at managing strategy," claims Rhinesmith. "The only thing we have to do in the strategy area is help executives redefine the competition. We think our competitors are in Japan, but in reality many of them are in Korea, Brazil, and the new Western Europe.

"We also need to help executives learn to manage decentralized, multicentered, flat-layered organizations. To do this, executives need to standardize the way they gather, process, and distribute information—where it comes from and how their computer systems are set up to manage it. This will ultimately mean a change in corporate culture. It's impossible to talk about globalizing executives without changing corporate cultures to be more global.

"We need to teach executives to manage multinational teams and alliances. We've been teaching teambuilding for years, but now we have to add the cultural dimension—what it's like to manage a multicultural team.

"I think one of the greatest challenges for executives will be the shift from managing competition to managing alliances with former competitors. Forming alliances will have the power to change a company's position on a world scale. After being number one for years, you'll wake up one morning and find you've become number three because two giants have merged against you.

"Finally I think you have to teach executives personal effectiveness—how to work across cultures, how to adjust to change, how to tolerate ambiguity. We have the methods and the technology for this but we need to use them in a new global context.

"The framework I use suggests you teach these new skills over a couple of years using different kinds of methodologies. It's not just a behavioral course; it's not just a cognitive course. In some areas we know what we're doing; in some areas the training profession needs to develop new paradigms and new training approaches.

"I think the biggest impediment to developing global effectiveness is that HRD people don't understand what global really means and don't have enough corporate methodologies to teach it, strengthen it, and develop it in their managers and in the culture. But I think it's doable. I'm very excited and optimistic about the opportunities this opens for the HRD profession in the 1990s."

The Basics

Doyle suggests that future executives need some "come-to-the-party skills." They include: how to teach on the run while making risky and instant decisions; how to be the chief learner in the corporation; and how to get people to take risks, to care, to be less arrogant, and to tell the truth without denial or oversimplification.

"I believe executives also need skills for contextual thinking—seeing the organization against the political, social, technological, or global background in which it operates." Columbia's Warner Burke adds, "It's not enough to have the right goals and the strategies to get to the right place. You also need the ability to get there in the face of a lot of uncertainty."

The Pitfalls

Thinking that one size fits all executive development is dangerous, asserts Doyle. "What do we mean by global companies? What is our ideal model of a global executive? Maybe we need multiple pathways to develop that model. Maybe we need different models for developing executives in different cultures based on their needs."

"What always worked at home may fail abroad," warns Adler. "We must invent ways to train young people and senior managers about global matters that do not simply use domestic frameworks. A study of strategic alliances among

North American, Japanese, and European companies found that American companies did not fare as well as their counterparts. Why? Because Japanese companies outlearned American companies in two areas: individual and organizational learning. Individual Americans working directly with the Japanese learned less than their counterparts, and the U.S. organizations learned little from their returning expatriate managers."

No Blueprint

The conventional picture of the executive—American style—is beginning to blur as the ability to command and control everything and everyone becomes impossible and unproductive. Captains of industry are evolving into something more like movie directors or orchestra conductors. Some, with a new concern for ethics and humanism in the workplace, are looking downright priestly. What is most clear is that there is no blueprint for this person.

"What would be the most distinctive difference between the executive of the year 2000 and today?" asks John Humphrey, CEO of The Forum Corporation. "More adaptability, multidimensional thinking, and the ability to impel people toward a vision. There are no rules for developing such a person, and the next 10 years will be a voyage of discovery for executives and executive developers, requiring new skills for both."

Executive, Know Thyself

Some of the challenges facing executives will call for a degree of psychic flexibility rare among today's corporate bosses. Future executives will have many more opportunities to cope with the unforeseen, admit failure, live with ambiguity, and test their sense of self.

The reinvented executive of the next decade will need to look inward as well as outward. Along with the big picture of how a company fits into a global economy, tomorrow's executive will need sharper personal insights in order to succeed, according to Warner Burke. He says, "A successful executive is one who is relatively self-aware. Our recent study shows that successful executives are more self-aware than their less successful counterparts. They are better at understanding their values."

Self-awareness will have to extend to what an executive doesn't know, claims DiStefano. "Past strengths can be future weaknesses but the key is learning which is which. Executives will have to know a lot more about a lot more things but they're going to be a lot less sure of what they know. For me that translates into a need for humility and a need to learn. Developing those two things in executives will be a challenge."

Badi Foster sees a spiritual dimension to executive development that is difficult to deal with because of the language attached to spirituality. "The only language we know how to use in the spiritual realm is religious language or poetry, so we're handicapped. But you can't be coherent in the act of transformation unless you have a clear notion of your transpersonal relationships. We don't have a way to deal with that."

Trends in Executive Development

Many surveys confirm that tomorrow's executive will need a new set of skills. The 35 participants in ASTD's Executive Development Seminar came up with a set of current and future executive traits (Table 2–1) and a skill model for the new global executive (Table 2–2).

If executives have a lot to learn, the amount of executive development seems likely to increase in American companies. ASTD surveyed a sample of *Fortune* 500 companies and found that, in the majority of them, senior managers and executives spend only one to five days a year in development and training programs. Much of it takes place outside the company in university or other external programs, and the content most likely to be covered concerns leadership and quality.

Robert DeSio, of National Technological University, is concerned that executives take so little interest in the process of learning—their own and others'—within their companies. "I would like to see executives more involved in learning in their companies. Considering that employers are spending $120 billion a year on training—more than the country spends on higher education—I'm concerned about executives' lack of involvement in the process. It's still a struggle to have training and education made part of corporate strategy."

Where will executive development go in the next 10 years? ASTD's governors believe that, with companies searching for global markets and striving to serve customers worldwide, it is likely that more of them will add a global aspect to their training and development, especially at the executive level. In addition, the growing demand for visionary leadership and for new kinds of thinking at the top will further change the complexion of executive development.

Commenting on promising changes in executive development that he has seen in companies, Juechter mentioned the following: less frequent, but bigger promotions, with a plan for making sure executives learn from each assignment; more opportunities to work in relatively unstructured teams whose output is critical to the success of the enterprise; frequent opportunities to interact two or three levels up in the organization; and interactions that reaffirm faith in the common man or woman.

"Senior executives have to meet the challenge of seeing the organization as a whole in the context of its multiple, external environments," cautions Juechter. "I would include in that group anyone with the title of vice president—anyone who needs to see the organization from the president's wholistic perspective and yet operate his or her own unit.

"Imagine a company as a sphere moving through time, interacting with all kinds of external environments as it goes. The economic, the technical, the political, the natural, and the social environments all make up the external context for an organization. Thinking about this particular cosmos is an intellectual task of a high order. The challenge is to develop that kind of thinking in executives.

TABLE 2–1
Executive Traits Now and in the Future

Current Traits	Future Traits
• All knowing	• Leader as learner
• Domestic vision	• Global vision
• Predicts the future from the past	• Intuits the future
• Caring for individuals	• Caring for institutions and individuals
• Owns the vision	• Facilitates the visions of others
• Uses power	• Uses power plus facilitation
• Dictates goals and methods	• Specifies processes
• Alone at the top	• Part of an executive team
• Values order	• Accepts the paradox of order amid chaos
• Monolingual	• Multicultural
• Inspires the trust of boards and shareholders	• Inspires the trust of owners, customers, and employees

"We have a model for this that has been operating successfully for four or five centuries—the practice of raising royalty to be in charge and to be responsible from day one. Companies accomplish something like this by giving people multiple assignments, but I wonder how many really put out a challenge to executives to think about the organization in relation to its environment."

Juechter advises that part of the design for executive assignment ought to include making sure the executives are stretched in their thinking and that they come away with a much larger picture of the organization than they started with. He also suggests that executives learn to challenge themselves in each assignment with something beyond survival and success.

Head Start

Some companies already have programs in place to develop global executives. However, most of the programs reported to ASTD's governors were new, and many were in the planning stage, suggesting that executive development with a global focus is still rare.

TABLE 2–2
A Skill Model for the New Global Executive

- Skills for understanding global business opportunities
- Skills for setting an organization's direction, for creating vision, mission, and purpose
- Skills for implementing the vision, mission, and purpose
- Skills for personal understanding and effectiveness

Some companies, such as Colgate Palmolive and Cray Research, give executives expatriate assignments to boost their global awareness. Colgate's Donna McNamara says her company tries to give executives worldwide experience. "We can't look at the issue of executive development without considering it in a global context. At Colgate we help senior technical executives deal with key variables and make decisions in a global marketplace," McNamara states.

Aetna has recently assessed the development of its executives in international jobs as a first step toward building a development plan for them. Aetna then hopes to establish a deliberate system of promotions and rotations between domestic and international assignments.

Even a company like Bethlehem Steel, with all of its operations based in the United States and few export sales, includes global competitiveness in the content of its executive development programs, reports Merlin Davidson, director of human resources. Chemical Bank, says William Linderman, vice president for corporate education, conducts multicultural development programs that set forth the culture at Chemical and define diversity of values and norms.

Jerry Tucker, manager of corporate education for GTE, reports these activities: adding global competitiveness to the content of courses for senior people, tailoring education for local business units, providing live experience as well as case studies, and forming partnerships with top-notch, credible college faculty.

To help executives broaden their horizons from domestic operations to global thinking, the seminar participants recommend supporting formal training for executives with some of these practices:

- Rotating junior-level vice presidents in global assignments.
- Including younger employees in cross-national task forces.
- Sending executives to visit key competitors in other countries.
- Sending executives to study foreign companies in the United States.
- Teaching foreign languages on a just-in-time basis.

- Offering reentry programs for executives returning from foreign assignments.
- Developing worldwide electronic study groups.

When developing global skills among executives, experts caution against confining them to a few people at the top of the company. They see a need for a common company language when discussing global business opportunities. Global awareness should not be the exclusive domain of people on expatriate assignments, they say.

Work Ahead

"We have to work harder to understand the new role of executives—especially its global aspects," claims Bill Yeomans, a consultant in executive development who works with multinational companies. "We have to identify executives' developmental needs and find ways to meet them.

"HRD people must provide stronger leadership in getting top management to realize that the job of the executive has changed, and that specific things need to be done to prepare people to be effective executives. Experience is no longer enough, because the work of keeping a company competitive in today's global economy is new; it wasn't there for the executive to learn on the way up.

"We know that companies invest billions in training their people but, unfortunately, that investment tapers off at the top of the company. People at executive levels or heading there are often seen as beyond the need for development. That just does not make sense from a business standpoint today. Organizations must start putting at least as many resources behind developing executives as they do training middle managers and first-line supervisors.

"A few companies are beginning to make real breakthroughs in executive development. We have to learn from them and apply their successful methods across the board in American business."

Reinventing the CEO

A study entitled *21st Century Report: Reinventing the CEO* by Korn/Ferry International and Columbia University's Graduate School of Business attempts to define the ideal characteristics of tomorrow's CEOs. It queried 1,500 businesspeople in 20 countries, who told researchers that the CEO of the year 2000 will be "a person of vision and a master strategist, capable of winning battles even before they begin."

The future chief executive must be a leader, says the report, inspiring managers to implement an optimistic corporate vision. The symbolic role of the corporate leader will be just as important as traditional business skills.

The survey asked respondents to evaluate 11 areas of expertise, 21 personal characteristics, and 17 areas of management style, as they exist today and in terms of their importance for the future. Human resource management scored number two in a ranking of the top 10 areas of expertise for the future.

Concerning management styles, the respondents ranked these five as most important: conveys vision of the company's future, links compensation to performance, emphasizes ethics, communicates frequently with employees, and promotes training and development.

Asked to rank the importance of specific formal training for CEOs, respondents produced this list: public speaking, dealing with the media, foreign languages (ranked very important by everyone but the Americans), and personal computer and telecommunications training.

The report on the survey noted that "the corporate leader of the 21st century must understand and accurately interpret the rapidly changing business environment. Only a CEO possessing a rare mental flexibility—a person able to understand, anticipate, and exploit perpetual change—will be capable of running a corporation dependent upon products (and even markets) that are as transient as cherry blossoms." Among the report's policy recommendations was the following: emphasize training and development for all managers, but especially for potential chief executives. The researchers predict that "the shortage of talented executives with the preparation necessary to run global companies may reach crisis proportions by the year 2000."

Critical Issues for CEOs

Chief Executive magazine polled 1,492 chairpersons and presidents of corporations about how they see the next 10 years. Of the CEOs who responded, 48 percent represent midsize companies, 38 percent are from small firms, and 12 percent run large corporations.

Most say they have a well-defined view of the future and that this vision is largely understood throughout their companies. The survey suggests that this is more true of larger corporations than it is of smaller ones.

These CEOs saw improving employee productivity and achieving financial growth as less imperative than improving market share and expanding product offerings. If finance and legal were the route to the top during the last decade, these CEOs expect it will be marketing and sales during the next. U.S. economic performance is their chief worry as is the return of increased inflation. International competitiveness appears somewhat less threatening as CEOs anticipate having fewer problems being targeted by foreign industries and having better luck in overseas markets. (Reported in *The Strategist*, a publication of Decision Processes International, Westport, Connecticut.)

Corporate executives need to know how to recruit competent global employees, open a sales office or a manufacturing plant in another country, and how to deal with currency fluctuations. Lawrence Tuller's book, *Going Global*, is a reference guide for anyone beginning to look at opportunities in markets outside the United States. "To take advantage of global opportunities, a company must go beyond exporting," says Tuller, "to thinking globally."[6] The book's broad coverage acquaints the novice with the risks and opportunities in various markets and where to get information about them. He also provides information on how and where to get financing, how to ship products and clear customs, and the tax implications of operating overseas. Tuller covers information on six important business areas: market opportunities, personnel recruitment, legal and accounting information, financing, selling and delivery procedures, and risk management. To obtain answers to questions in these areas, he outlines seven good sources, including the U.S. Department of Commerce.

EXECUTIVE MANAGEMENT COMMITMENT

Training managers must be educators seeking ways to raise awareness of cultural issues in decision making. If there is little top-management commitment to global issues and executive management is slow to commit resources for training, human resource directors can arrange a trip to allow top-level management from the United States to travel to global sites and meet with government officials and subordinates at that site. The push to sensitize global thinking at the top can be initiated by an interested individual in a global subsidiary of a large corporation. Major customers can also request a visit from top management where customers can share their concerns and insight with top executives. Companies who have planned such visits report that it proved to be a real mind-opener that has greatly increased top-management commitment to global training. The key is to be sure the trip is more in-depth and longer than the usual two-day red-carpet stop.

Developing failure scenarios is another tactic training managers can use to obtain corporate commitment to training. In presenting proposals for global training, trainers must be able to articulate specific failure scenarios. Clarifying time, place, and probable actors makes a presentation more powerful. Sources from within the company can help the training manager identify and accurately depict these scenarios. When executives see the costs of these failures, they will more fully understand the importance of global training.

TOP-MANAGEMENT DEVELOPMENT

In summary, corporate training managers must help executives develop skills and increase their ability to lead global corporations. Executive seminars and briefings should emphasize:

- Changing thinking patterns and strategies from a domestic focus to a global mindset.
- Managing uncertainty and fear while constantly adapting to change.
- Combining the many cultures of the corporate workforce into a unique global organizational culture.
  –Developing the desire to learn from a culturally diverse workforce.
  –Developing the ability to work with people of other cultures as equals.
- Learning how to collaborate with partners worldwide and to manage global teams and alliances.

Global training for top management must incorporate a body of cultural knowledge, an openness to other cultures, and cultural empathy. It must also focus on adaptive, problem-solving skills for both managers and employees. These skills encompass a flexibility that will enable them to redefine strategies and reinvent structures within the global organization. Executives must be committed to investing time and money in their own development and in a corporate global training effort.

To borrow a popular phrase from many years ago, global training is *where the rubber meets the road.* As company executives and employees put their multicultural knowledge and skills into action, the practical value and impact of global training will be evident as the corporation continues to expand markets and operations worldwide.

Chapter Three

Creating a Global Training Strategy

There are many neighborhoods in the global village.

—Anthony Carnevale , *America in the New Economy*

In his book, *Total Global Strategy*, George S. Yip explains that there is more to being a global corporation than just opening and staffing offices in many countries.[1] Most transnational companies are not changing fast enough to respond to the new reality of open global markets, the need to coordinate activities within these markets, and the necessity of an adequate global strategy. Yip believes global organizations must operate by managing their businesses on an integrated, worldwide basis rather than in a loosely connected federation of subsidiaries. Successful global managers know the value of a total global strategy that can improve quality and customer service, reduce costs, and increase leverage against competitors. A truly competitive global company focuses its strategy on four major factors: organizational structure, management activities and processes, people, and culture.

Stephen H. Rhinesmith, in his article, "An Agenda for Globalization," also emphasizes that the basic building block for effective globalization is corporate strategy.[2] However, for many companies, strategic planning is still an enigma or, at best, done on a small scale for short-term goals. It is no wonder that strategic planning for employee development concerning global issues is almost unheard of for U. S. companies. Most non-U. S. companies have also avoided developing global training strategies. As corporations continue to globalize, special attention to global training strategy issues will emerge as a critical factor.

ALIGN THE TRAINING STRATEGY WITH THE COMPANY STRATEGY

No longer is it sufficient to sporadically offer a few cultural courses for expatriates. This Band-Aid approach will not support the global corporation. The training strategy of the global company must align itself with the global corporate strategy. While training can supply the motivation, knowledge, and skills needed for improvement, it cannot be effective unless what is learned is consistent with management practices. Training should not precede a careful examination and development of corporate global strategy.

NCR is a global company with more than 300 domestic facilities and more than 600 international facilities in more than 120 countries. Currently, the company is in the third year of a five-year plan that will redirect all of its training. NCR emphasizes that it must be clear how programs will help the company manufacture its products and sell them at a profit.[3] Ralph Catalanello and John Redding stated in December 1989 that the literature of recent years has enthusiastically extolled the importance of tying training to strategic business planning. "Strategy-linked training may be essential to the success of contemporary firms challenged by increasing global competition, accelerating technological change, and shifting workforce demographics. In fact, several leading organizations, including Motorola, General Electric, and Hewlett-Packard, credit recent business success to training."[4]

FOLLOW A PROCESS TO DEVELOP A STRATEGY

Once the corporate global strategy is known and understood, a training strategy can be developed. The purpose of the strategy is to produce a vision and plan for the future. It should be used as a tool rather than viewed as an exercise that has to be accomplished once a year.

The strategic planning process should be a systematic one. The following are some guidelines for this process, which consists of seven interrelated steps:[5]

1. Determine the organization's values.

2. Create a global training mission.

3. Examine internal and external environments that affect the training.

4. Identify training goals and objectives.

5. Identify action steps to accomplish the plan.

6. Test strategic goals and objectives.

7. Design a system to obtain feedback about the plan's results.

STEP 1—DETERMINE THE ORGANIZATION'S VALUES

An organization's values define its culture. By identifying the values, you have a picture of managers' and employees' feelings, beliefs, and attitudes, which are powerful forces in an organization. It is important to keep these forces in mind when developing a strategy because they influence its effectiveness. When a corporation is global, its culture is influenced by the cultures of the countries in which it operates, and this multiculturalism is a critical factor in developing its strategy.

Questions used in identifying the organization's values are those targeted to managers and employees, such as:

Managers

- What are your beliefs about how the business operates?
- What kind of performance do you expect of your employees?
- How are people rewarded for performance?
- How do you communicate with employees?
- What expectations do you have regarding your employees' behavior?
- How do people make decisions in the organization?
- How do values differ in those countries in which the company does business?

Employees

- Do you feel that the company prepares you to deliver the highest service to customers?

- Do you feel that the organization positively rewards work efforts?
- How do employees (in non-U. S. countries) feel about having U. S. managers?
- How do employees in the United States feel about having non-U.S. managers?
- Do you feel valued and appreciated?

Defining your organization's culture helps you determine the kind of training that will develop corporate values important to the success of your corporate strategy. William Wiggenhorn, Motorola's corporate vice president for training and education, says, "Culture in a corporation is partly a question of history and of common language—a form of tribal storytelling. At Motorola, for example, we believe in taking risks. Our history shows it was one of the things that made us great. Telling those stories creates a tradition of risk, invests it with value, and encourages young people to go out and do the same."[6] An example of a global corporation's training vision and values is provided by Gordon Bennett, global training manager for ASEA Brown Boveri's Process Automation in Figure 3–1.[7]

STEP 2—CREATE A GLOBAL TRAINING MISSION

After you have defined values, establish the training function's mission. As you think about your mission, keep the corporate mission in mind. Your mission should support the corporate mission.

A mission is a statement of your function's purpose. It provides focus and direction, serving as a guide to the development of goals and objectives. The challenge to training functions in global companies is to create mission statements that are unifying and, at the same time, broad enough to include the diversity within the company. The following are elements to consider including in your statement:

- Your group's name.
- Your group's role in the organization.
- The population your group serves.
- The interventions to be employed by training programs.
- The outcomes desired as a result of the interventions.

An example of a mission statement that includes all these criteria is: The corporate training division of ABC Global provides educational and

FIGURE 3–1

ASEA Brown Boveri's (ABB) Process Automation Global/Local Training Vision and Values

---

1. ACTION-ORIENTED ENVIRONMENT
- Create and promote a proactive environment of achievement in which action, initiative, and responsible risk taking are integral to the operation.

2. PERSONAL QUEST FOR EXCELLENCE
- Instill pride and commitment. Empower people to manage themselves and take responsibility for their actions and results.

- Develop self-initiated, goal-directed, and results-oriented individuals who see their working environment as a place of challenging and developmental opportunities.

- Give recognition and rewards for high achievers.

3. MARKETING AND OPERATING STRENGTHS
- Recognize and fulfill the training needs and requirements of the client/customer as an extension of the sales function.

- Link the day-to-day activities to clearly established customer and ABB-Process Automation organizational requirements.

- Respond to the worldwide training marketplace requirements through innovation, creativity, and excellence that consistently exceed industry training standards.

- Conduct ongoing research to create continual opportunities for superior approaches to client/customer operational needs.

- Promote and establish partnership relationships with clients and associates.

- Integrity is the foundation for all our actions with respect to clients and employees in our open communication and actions.

4. TRAINING EFFECTIVENESS
- Support external, internal, and worldwide organizational needs with standard and specialized training products.

- Provide consistent quality and content of training products globally, locally adapted to accommodate area-unique training requirements.

- Achieve maximum training effectiveness through continual evaluation of past students' capabilities to perform their jobs.

- Make ongoing modifications/upgrades by reviewing leading-edge training technologies/techniques for maximum skills/knowledge transference.

5. FINANCIAL
- Operate the training function as a business by supporting systems orders obtained.

- Be financially self-sufficient for cash flow, capital needs for growth regarding revenues and gross margins.

6. CULTURE
- Establish a culture that encourages and supports:

  — Enthusiasm
  — High energy
  — Respect
  — Integrity
  — Ethics
  — Rewards
  — Development
  — Entrepreneurship
  — Fun

---

training services that support the corporate strategy. Our division does this through programs that enhance employees' ability to contribute to the growth, efficiency, competitiveness, and profitability of the company in global markets.

In *A Manager's Guide to Globalization*, Rhinesmith states that it is not easy to create a mission that is meaningful to people from various cultures and different social, political, and economic viewpoints from across the globe.[8] "One reason it is so difficult to achieve a culturally acceptable global corporate mission," he continues, "is that a mission statement is the connection of a corporation to the values of a society and its workforce. A global corporation by definition operates in many different societies with a multicultural workforce. This means that its mission must be stated in a way that is attractive to the greatest number of people from the greatest number of cultural, social, economic, and political backgrounds."

STEP 3—EXAMINE INTERNAL AND EXTERNAL ENVIRONMENTS THAT AFFECT THE TRAINING

The next step in establishing a strategic plan is to analyze two environments: internal and external. This analysis will help you:

- Determine the function's strengths and weaknesses (internal) and opportunities and constraints (external).
- Determine situations that might aid and/or prevent the accomplishment of your mission.

Consider asking questions about the following internal and external environments:

Internal

- Financial condition.
- Managerial abilities and attitudes.
- Facilities.
- Staffing size and quality.
- The training function's competitive position.
- The training function's organizational image.
- Centralized versus decentralized structure.
- Distance between work teams.
- Language differences.
- Cultural issues.

External

- Economic condition of the organization in the various countries in which it is located.
- Legal and political realities within the various countries.
- Social and cultural values.
- Technological state.
- Availability of resources.
- Competitive structure of the organization.

From this analysis, you can make adjustments to compensate for weaknesses and constraints and to build on strengths and opportunities. For example, let's say that your company has an aggressive corporate mission to grow internationally. Your analysis of internal and external environments reveals, however, that management is not clear about its role in the globalization of training and development of employees. Part of your training strategy, then, might be to address this issue. Executive and management training that informs and motivates will be important to achieve management understanding and to strengthen commitment to training. A vital beginning element of your strategy may be to conduct executive briefing—perhaps in the form of retreats or special programs that include topics such as multicultural management, global business issues, and the importance of global training.

Conducting such an environmental analysis is very important in surfacing the information that helps you to be proactive and to intervene when necessary with educational and motivational programs.

STEP 4—IDENTIFY TRAINING GOALS AND OBJECTIVES

Next, think about your mission as you develop training goals and objectives. The purpose of each goal and objective should be to accomplish the training function's mission and to create focus on what is to be done.

A strategic goal should be:

- Specific: Make the goal clear and easy to understand.
- Measurable: Use as standards for measuring a goal.
- Agreed upon: Get agreement from your client that the goal will meet the identified need.

- Realistic: Consider adjusting the deadline and/or resources if the goal is not realistic.
- Written: Provide the necessary structure and focus to gain commitment from the training function's employees.

While goals provide direction for the program, objectives provide information about how a goal is to be implemented. Essentially, objectives are specific tasks required to accomplish a strategic goal.

Like strategic goals, objectives must also be specific, measurable, agreed upon, realistic, and written. Additionally, each objective should identify key participants and resources.

STEP 5—IDENTIFY ACTION STEPS TO ACCOMPLISH THE PLAN

Once the strategic goals and objectives are developed, an action plan should be designed that states how they will be implemented. Basic questions to be answered are:

- How will the strategic plan be implemented?
- Who will direct the implementation?
- What is the deadline for implementation?
- How will the plan's success be measured?

Let's look at two strategic goals, objectives, and action plans as identified by the training function of a global company:

Goal #1: In July 1993, corporate training will initiate an activity that ensures the regional training directors understand and are committed to the global training strategy.

Objective: Conduct a meeting of regional training managers in July to develop understanding of the training strategy activities and identify responsibilities.

Action Plan:

Due Date	Activity
7/93	Convene a meeting of the training managers from the various countries in which we do business.

- Each team will review its training activities.
- Request and receive information on how many employees need basic training.
- Hold a round-table session to identify concerns and needs.
- Responsibility: Corporate training director.

Goal #2: Develop the required resources for curriculum needs.

Objectives: By the end of 1993, training managers will:
- Identify client groups needing training programs.
- Assess the basic job skills needed for programs.
- Prioritize course development.
- Identify work load requirements.

Action Plan:

Due Date	Activity
8/93	Conduct a survey and gather results to determine client groups needing programs.
11/93	Conduct a job skills analysis to assess the basic job skills needed for programs.
12/93	Prioritize course development.
12/93	Identify the work load requirements from: • Line training resources. • Corporate training resources. • Borrowed adjunct resources. • Contract resources. • New-hire resources added to the appropriate training team. • Responsibility: Each region's training director.

STEP 6—TEST STRATEGIC GOALS AND OBJECTIVES

The strategic plan should be visionary, but it should also be tested for realistic and obtainable goals and objectives in the light of constraints within the company. Some of the questions that should be considered in this phase are:

- What are the resources needed in our local global markets to accomplish our goals and objectives?
- If the resources are not available, how can they be acquired?
- What are the constraints in our local global markets that may keep us from achieving our goals and objectives?
- Can we decrease these constraints? If so, how?

STEP 7—DESIGN A SYSTEM TO OBTAIN FEEDBACK ABOUT THE PLAN'S RESULTS

To determine the success of your plan, you will need a system for getting information. The information you gather must be comprehensive enough to determine how future strategic plans must be modified and developed to succeed. Some of the questions you can ask yourself when designing your system are:

- How will you know when the strategic goals and objectives have been accomplished?
- How will you monitor the progress of your strategic plan?
- What alternative plans can be created if the initial plan fails?

CONCLUSIONS

American companies are moving toward globalization on several fronts, including integration of their global manufacturing and marketing operations, rapid transmission of information and technology across transnational borders, and the development and implementation of successful global campaigns and strategies. Training strategies that support these corporate plans are essential for the crucial development of global managers. As Richard P. Bergeman, vice president of human resources for CPC International, Inc. says, "When you talk about globalization, you're talking about resource allocation and the most efficient use of your resources. What more important resource is there than your human resources?"[9]

Chapter Four

Designing Guidelines for Global Training

*The ability to function effectively in a multicultural environment is essen-
tial in today's world. Intercultural skills are the new survival skills, replac-
ing the ethnocentric response that protected our ancestors.*

—Margaret D. Pusch
President of Intercultural Press

D esigning training courses for the multicultural workforce poses a distinct
challenge. Instructional designers know that they cannot simply translate the training material into a variety of languages. They must consider the
program design—each word and each activity—from the standpoint of
impact on the specific culture. These considerations are not only difficult to
address, but the process is extremely time intensive. The design team should
include not only trainers who are competent in instructional design technology but should also include members from the targeted culture group.

APPROACHES TO TRAINING DESIGN

Different schools of thought on designing training in the United States and
abroad compete with and sometimes contradict the practices instructional
designers have experienced in the field. One school of thought seeks to provide universal models to fit virtually every training situation. Another seeks

to use local culture in training as a starting point before beginning any instructional design process. Both of these approaches and other models are all representative of what constitutes an eclectic approach.

With increasing trends toward globalization, more human and commercial transactions are being conducted across national boundaries, thus presenting new challenges in cross-cultural training. Human transactions are based on seeking a common understanding despite individual differences. In the United States, trainers are fortunate to be able to provide training that draws on a shared background. When working outside the United States, they must keep in mind that each culture has a unique background with different assumptions, methods, and modes of communication as well as inherent capacities and limitations.

Unfortunately, misunderstandings are likely to occur because of differences in psychological and linguistic interpretations. Ideally, training should be developed to accommodate these differences. In working with so many cultures, it is important to have approaches that strike a universal balance. Successful instructional design (ID) models have been developed and appear to have global cultural applications. Instruction Systems Development (ISD) has taken on a life of its own with the myriad permutations that Figure 4–1 outlines.[1] Performance-based training goes beyond simple training by looking at the operating system parameters that affect human performance. More recently, research and applications from cognitive psychology reveal more appropriate designs that encourage evaluating instruction from the perspective of learner development.

Despite these new developments, it is evident that cross-cultural training is sometimes deficient. A 1990 World Bank study found that, after years of providing employees with technical assistance, the transfer of expertise was not resulting in the expected improvement of individual skills or the enhanced capacity of institutions. Training in many aid-sponsored efforts lacked cultural sensitivity as well as grounding in basic design principles. Many experts who were involved with technology transfer were poorly prepared to interact and deliver training. Many did not receive appropriate predeparture intercultural training, and fewer still had the design skills to provide flexible responses in training. For example, the strong task orientation of Western culture does not play well in many Asian cultures that regard establishing good rapport as the first order of business.

To address this deficiency, this chapter first presents ideas of what culture is and how cultures differ so that seasoned American trainers going abroad will have a better understanding of the challenges they face. Then conceptual

FIGURE 4–1

Interservice Procedures for Instructional Systems Development Model

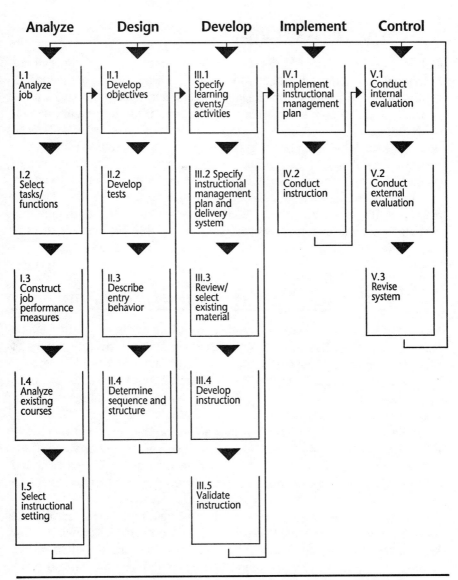

Source: J. F. Wedman and M. Tessmer, "The Layers of Necessity ID Model," *Performance and Instruction*, 29, no. 41, (April 1990).

models of human thought processes, which should be considered in designing training programs, are presented.

WHAT IS CULTURE?

Culture is a group's collective intellectual environment. It is everything individuals are exposed to that formulates the way they experience life. Culture includes notions from relatives, peers, and institutions. It includes concepts of childhood, work, friendship, disease, death, history, art, natural environment, language, symbols, etiquette, and more (see Figure 4–2).[2] The problem with defining and understanding culture is that, like a fish in water, it surrounds you at all times. Human beings in a new culture could be compared to fish out of water. Fortunately, however, humans are able to understand and adapt, and so the consequences are not nearly so dire. Trainers can never fully appreciate a culture, unless they begin to live it. Being ignorant about another culture, however, is not acceptable nor possible if training is to be successful.

LANGUAGE—AN EXPRESSION OF CULTURE

Language is among the most conspicuous expressions of culture. Aside from the obvious differences, vocabularies are built on the experiences of the users. For example, speakers of Arabic have only one word for ice: *telg*. This word applies equally to ice cube, hail, and snow. On the other hand, the Eskimo languages have a number of descriptive words describing the quality of snow itself.

In Japanese, the word for *individualism* has negative connotations, reflecting that culture's regard for the collective good over the value of the self. In contrast, the word *individualism* is revered in the United States. If trainers compliment a person from Japan and one from the United States on his or her individualism, they can expect different reactions.

Because communication is so critical in the training process, learning the local language is encouraged. When time does not permit, knowing a few key phrases and using them appropriately may open doors as well as minds. Salutatory greetings, farewells, and courtesies indicate a desire to reach across the divide. It is amazing how quickly trainers can amass a small, working vocabulary in another language if they are willing to take the risk

FIGURE 4–2
The Iceberg Conception of the Nature of Culture

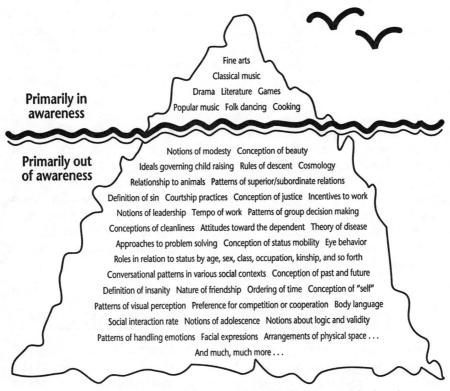

Primarily in awareness

Fine arts
Classical music
Drama   Literature   Games
Popular music   Folk dancing   Cooking

Primarily out of awareness

Notions of modesty   Conception of beauty
Ideals governing child raising   Rules of descent   Cosmology
Relationship to animals   Patterns of superior/subordinate relations
Definition of sin   Courtship practices   Conception of justice   Incentives to work
Notions of leadership   Tempo of work   Patterns of group decision making
Conceptions of cleanliness   Attitudes toward the dependent   Theory of disease
Approaches to problem solving   Conception of status mobility   Eye behavior
Roles in relation to status by age, sex, class, occupation, kinship, and so forth
Conversational patterns in various social contexts   Conception of past and future
Definition of insanity   Nature of friendship   Ordering of time   Conception of "self"
Patterns of visual perception   Preference for competition or cooperation   Body language
Social interaction rate   Notions of adolescence   Notions about logic and validity
Patterns of handling emotions   Facial expressions   Arrangements of physical space . . .
And much, much more . . .

Just as nine tenths of an iceberg is out of sight (below the water line), so is nine tenths of culture out of conscious awareness. The out-of-awareness part of culture has been termed "deep culture."

Reprinted with permission from "A Workshop on Cultural Differences," developed by Indrei Fatiu and Irene Rodgers. Published in *AFS Orientation Handbook*, Vol. IV, 1984.

and use what they know of the language with native speakers. Nevertheless, American trainers are often reluctant to engage in this process because of the potential for embarrassment. People in other cultures, however, are most eager to assist the sojourner through the process. Global training assign-ments that span several years make language acquisition easier as the trainer develops an ear for the language as well as a larger working vocabulary. One caution, though: any attempt to conduct training in another language should be taken very seriously. Academic learning of a language or through an expatriate who has not actively kept abreast of language nuances could turn a training session or a diplomatic event into a major embarrassment. Remember the Polish translator from the United States who indicated that an American president *lusted* for beautiful Polish women? Only qualified trans-lators should be hired in other countries. Likewise, early preparation is required to convert a training program from one culture to another.

Although linguistic differences may appear minor, they can be significant for the trainer. For example, the Irish and British are thought to share English as a common language with Americans. Yet, understanding the cultural implications of linguistic format and structure are very important in prepar-ing presentations for these cousins of the English language. The long literary tradition in Europe has provided the European counterparts with a rich, high-ly descriptive working vocabulary that may be sensed by Americans as stuffy or overbearing. In contrast, U.S. training productions may appear to be simplistic or poorly articulated.

CULTURE AND NONVERBAL COMMUNICATION

Another form of communication that is culturally specific is body language. Trainers must be aware of body language to understand members of another culture, to practice proper etiquette, and to avoid embarrassing situations. For example, South Asians commonly roll their heads from side to side to signify an understanding or concurrence with a person speaking. This can cause considerable confusion for unaware trainers, who may interpret it as a sign of negation.

Similarly, the rolling eyes of Japanese trainees are an indication of think-ing rather than a lack of attentiveness. A respectful greeting in Japan and other East Asian countries is to bow. The lower a person bows, the more respect he or she is showing.

In various cultures around the world, trainers need to exercise care regarding their feet. In East Asian countries, trainers can experience consid-erable embarrassment if they wear shoes inside a house, temple, or even in an office setting. In Thailand, the feet are the basest part of the body, and it is offensive to point with one's feet. Similarly, in Saudi Arabia, it is an insult to show a person the bottom of one's shoe. An unseasoned American may find these practices odd. However, trainers can be assured that they are equally as peculiar as Americans exchanging handshakes, asking "How do you do?" or making persistent inquiries into the health and emotional condition of strangers, who are consistently "Fine." It is essential for trainers to learn the basic etiquette and appropriate physical conduct of the country they are visiting. Visiting trainers should clarify unfamiliar customs with a local company employee in whom they have confidence before the training session.

An exan   situations is illustrated ii   to explain to a
Japanese   of Mount Fuji at
night wi   xplained that the
flash pro   vould not illumi-
nate the   ill take a picture
of Fuji-s   to take a picture.
For her,   d admiration for
the este   their goals, but
because   eans were different. And   ish for taking the
picture,   own the man for
not usin;

The   dbook, a useful resource for cross-cultural sensitivity, provides another good example of how people from different cultures may draw erroneous judgments from misinterpretations.[3] An American girl studying in France concluded that the French are "...pretty nice, but they are all hypocrites. They kiss you on both cheeks, as if they really like you. But it doesn't mean a damn thing!" Her judgment was based on the fact that, in the United States, kissing may communicate a close relationship, but in the student population in France, it means *hello* and nothing more. Unknowing French persons in the United States may find equally offensive the reaction of acquaintances to whom they apply *la bise* (the kiss). This illustrates the need for trainers to re-orient themselves when working with a new set of cultural assumptions.

Also, D. A. Ralston and others in a recent study indicate that factors such as the globalization of business procedures and technology have a modifying effect on many traditional practices.[4]

ADAPTATION OF TRAINING
TO LOCAL CONDITIONS

Effective trainers take into consideration local conditions when designing training. For example, they are aware that it is less meaningful to teach construction methods using wood in a desert country setting because wood is scarce in such areas.

Similarly, a trainer engaged in teaching the benefits of environmental protection in a country where pollution control laws are lax should stress environmental technologies that will save money and reduce problems in the long term.

Cross-cultural training for company employees needs to be correlated to specific training applications. Recommendations for the design and presentation of global training include:

1. Provide opportunities for the trainees to apply the material to their own cultural situation. Role-playing and case studies work well by relating real problems and possible solutions. This will prevent a common syndrome caused by an insensitive trainer who watches trainees take copious notes and expound on the themes taught but not be able to apply the themes to their needs. But in locations where there is no precedent for application of knowledge, trainees may not understand how to react when increased participation is indicated. Begin conservatively, then shift to more interactive designs.

2. Be empathetic to feedback from the trainees. Successful cross-cultural communication may be difficult in cultures that shun criticism or that ensure the comfort of participants through hospitality. Role plays and case studies enable the trainer to see how the participants have interpreted and reacted to the training. The trainer can then determine if the message is appropriate to the other culture and is being understood.

3. Look for opportunities to take advantage of cultural differences. For example, in an area where there is an antagonistic relationship between government and industry, designing training to bring those groups together may show that there is a common goal in cooperation. Show the participants how a certain concept is implemented in the trainer's culture and discuss the differences encountered. Opportunities such as these are appropriate for the U.S. trainer but are not for a local person.

4. Be sensitive to a culture's methods of learning and working. Some cultures may stress memorization, lists, logic, or cooperation. A trainer who does not understand a culture's learning styles will meet considerable frustration.

In Egypt, a trainer encountered a resistance to written examinations and learned that the Egyptians' ethic of cooperation rendered written tests inappropriate. Oral group exams proved useful in that situation. In some circumstances, methods of learning, thinking, and operating can be the most valuable lesson learned by the trainees or trainer. The newly democratized cultures are accustomed to doing business without the type of pluralism, caution, and negotiating terms found in most capitalist societies. Under these circumstances, a trainer may have difficulty getting students to debate issues. From an outsider's point of view, it appears that helping to develop these skills might be a most important objective of the training.

5. Learn about the local region and its technology. Know the educational level of the trainees. Work with the local people before beginning training. If the training is about factory safety, tour local factories. Ask the workers to present their views in their country on the training topic before you begin designing or presenting the training. The trainer may find that an exchange, rather than a transfer, of ideas is more appropriate.

6. Most important, remember that, as an outsider, the trainer will never fully understand the communication styles, methods, constraints, and assets of the culture. It is useful to try to understand and to discuss any gaps in understanding with the trainees. But trainers should be cautious in judging something as wrong; it may simply be different. A most effective way of avoiding this cultural pitfall is to train local trainers, preferably top practitioners in the field. Training local trainers to develop and present their own programs should be a major objective of global training.

American trainers must be prepared to address the challenge of working in new cultures. As sojourners in another culture, trainers should prepare themselves using books, periodicals, and cultural inventory checklists.[5] A more meaningful experience would be to attend one of the two- or three-day intercultural workshops that develop empathetic reactions to novel situations. Such workshops—presented by consulting firms experienced in crosscultural training—contrast U.S. culture and its own ambiguities with other cultures to create comparative models of understanding. Workshops that emphasize a dos and don'ts list are useful but not as enriching as those that provide models.

Other cultural learning resources are available from the U. S. Government. Background notes from the State Department and Country Profiles by the Central Intelligence Agency are available from the Government Printing Office. These documents can be ordered by mail from the Superintendent of Documents, U.S. Government Printing Office, Washington, DC 20402-9324 or by phone at (202) 783-3238. Embassies, consulates, and trade missions provide highly descriptive information about their respective countries. Other training resources are listed in Appendix A. Time permitting, one of the most meaningful experiences is to befriend a native from the culture the trainer is about to enter. Global organizations usually have employees on staff from different cultures. Larger universities host a number of foreign nationals, and members of international societies including ASTD can provide valuable contacts. In today's world there are many resources at a trainer's disposal requiring only a modest investment in time, so there is virtually no excuse for being unprepared.

THE RELATIONSHIP BETWEEN INSTRUCTION AND LEARNING

Traditional wisdom says that training has been successful if the trainer taught and the trainee learned. This dichotomy—the relationship between learning and instruction—is at the core of any training effort, in the United States or abroad. Let's look at several theoretical models that can help trainers understand the new tools needed for cross-cultural training.

THE ROLE OF CULTURE IN LEARNING

Research confirms that trainees construct and modify their understanding of the world as a result of experience with some help from instruction. Learners bring informational characteristics—their ideas, concepts, and beliefs developed over years in a specific culture—to the training session. Variations in individual interpretations are also seen, particularly in the cultures where individualism is valued. Figure 4–3 provides a general distribution model showing how these informational characteristics vary within a specific culture and how they are shared among other cultures. Shared elements in a particular culture constitute a cultural set that identifies the majority in the culture. The role of the instructional designer is to relate and modify this cultural set to new information and knowledge. When working across cultures, instructional designers should capitalize on the characteristics that are shared among cultures. This common ground is an effective departure for conducting training.

Geert Hofstede, in *Cultures and Organizations: Software of the Mind*, identifies culture through four dimensions that provide guidelines for

FIGURE 4–3

Culture as a Distribution of Characteristics—the "Cultural Set"

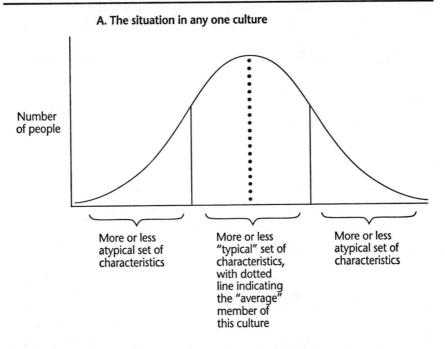

A. The situation in any one culture

Number of people

More or less atypical set of characteristics

More or less "typical" set of characteristics, with dotted line indicating the "average" member of this culture

More or less atypical set of characteristics

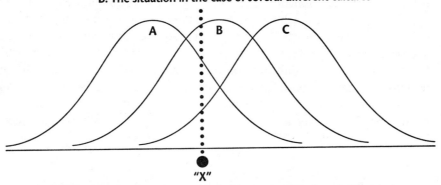

B. The situation in the case of several different cultures

A   B   C

"X"

Cultures A, B, and C are different in terms of some human characteristics, but similar in terms of others. Cultures A and C have the least in common, but they are not totally dissimilar. The individual "X" has a certain combination of characteristics denoted by the dotted line. He or she has much in common with Culture B, some in common with Culture A, and a little in common with Culture C.

Source: *AFS Orientation Handbook*, Vol. IV, 1984. Copyright AFS Intercultural Programs.

instructional design.[6] Each of the dimensions in Figure 4–4 provides a continuum on which a society anchors its cultural set. Although each of the dimensions holds meaning for the instructional designer, power distance and the masculinity-femininity dimensions are the most significant.

Power distance is the extent to which a society accepts power in institutions and people, and different cultures align with either high-power distance or low-power distance.

High-Power Distance	*Low-Power Distance*
• Formal relationships	• Largely informal
• High dependence	• Low dependence
• Teacher-centered	• Learner-centered
• Highly personal	• Impersonal
• Status emphasized	• Equality emphasized
• Fixed approach	• Variable approach
• Conformity	• Experimentation

Usually, individualistic cultures such as the United States, are toward the low end of the continuum and collective cultures tend toward the high end. This difference provides significant clues for the designer/trainer. For example, countries with high-power distance maximize individual status and are more comfortable with a known, well-laid out approach using a more formal teacher-learner relationship. The low-power distance countries minimize individual status and encourage experimenting as a way of learning. In high-power distance countries it is far better to use a conservative design approach before introducing more innovative participant-centered products. High-power distance cultures tolerate a number of interactive training designs as long as proprieties are observed. Although the Hofstede model provides an excellent macroperspective of numerous cultures, individual country profiles provide additional clues for designing instructional products for a specific culture.

APPLICATIONS FROM COGNITIVE SCIENCE

Knowledge of the human brain and its information-processing capabilities is relatively new. Cognitive science provides trainers with a better understanding of how they can relate thought processes to instructional design and training products. Understanding these fundamental processes can also improve

FIGURE 4–4
Representations Adapted from Geert Hofstede's Four Dimensions

POWER DISTANCE The extent to which the less powerful members of society accept that power is distributed unequally.

LOW
Low dependence needs
Inequality minimized
Hierarchy for convenience
Superiors accessible
All have equal rights
Change of revolution

HIGH
High dependence needs
Inequality accepted
Hierarchy needed
Superiors often inaccessible
Power-holders have privileges
Change by evolution

TASK-ORIENTED The dominance of achievement and success over caring for others and the quality of life.

LOW
Quality of life and serving
    others highly valued
Striving for consensus
Work in order to live
Small and slow are beautiful
Sympathy for the unfortunate
Men and women have
    overlapping roles
Intuition valued

HIGH
Ambitious and a need to excel
Tendency to polarize
Live in order to work
Big and fast are beautiful
Admiration for the achiever
Men and women have separate roles
Decisiveness valued

INDIVIDUALISM The importance of the role of the individual versus the role of the group.

LOW
"We" conscious
Relationships valued over the task
Fulfill the obligations of the group
Loss of "face," shame
Differing value standards

HIGH
"I" conscious
Private opinions
Fulfill obligations to one's self
Loss of self-respect, guilt
Universal value standards

UNCERTAINTY AVOIDANCE The extent to which people feel threatened by uncertain and unknown situations.

LOW
Relaxed, lower stress
Hard work not a virtue per se
Emotions not shown
Conflict and competition = fair play
Acceptance of dissent
Willingness to take risks
There should be few rules

HIGH
Anxiety, higher stress
Inner urge to work hard
Showing emotions accepted
Conflict is threatening
Need for consensus
Need to avoid failure
Need for laws and rules

Source: "International Passport Seminar," presented by Center for international training and education, 1992.

trainers' abilities to comprehend other cultures. Figure 4–5 provides key elements for an intercultural training system based on several cognitive models.

The role of memory appears to play a critical function in this processing operation. In his study of memory systems, E. Tulving provides a useful approach in proposing three different but interrelated memory systems—procedural, semantic, and episodic.[7]

- At the lowest level, procedural memory retains learned connections between a stimulus and response. An example of procedural memory is a driver pulling his car to the side of the road when he hears a siren.

- Semantic memory represents states of the world that are not perceptually present or expressed in another way—information that is present in various forms, such as concepts and heuristics that can be drawn on. An example of semantic memory is the driver's knowledge that the siren he hears symbolizes an emergency such as a fire or accident.

- Episodic memory is more culturally modified in that it depends on both semantic and procedural memory systems to form knowledge about personally experienced events. An example of episodic memory might be the driver's memory of a fire at a neighbor's house last week.

Figure 4–6 provides a useful model in contrasting the elements of memory and presenting instructional products that can be developed to bridge knowledge as well as cultural differences.

KNOWLEDGE ORGANIZATION

The organization of knowledge in memory is one of the central issues in cognitive science. Results in this area are directly applicable to training design. Knowledge is viewed as being organized in schemas—hierarchical network-like structures of concepts, their features, and their interrelationships. Higher skill levels are characterized by schemas that are more hierarchical, more highly elaborated, easier to access, and more automated. The highly developed schemas allow individuals to perform at ease in their culture and in particular jobs.[8] Routine examples of schemas are how to dress and act appropriately at a dinner or reception.

Ideally, training should be structured to promote optimal schema development. For example, trainers should:

- Relate new information to existing knowledge schemas.
- Organize material following its conceptual structure.

FIGURE 4–5
Key Elements for an Intercultural Education/Training System

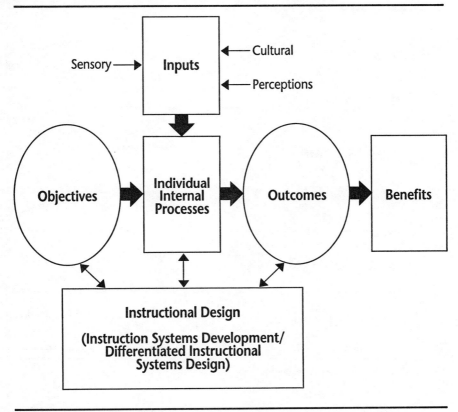

Source: Peter Beckschi, director of training, World Environment Center.

- Teach prototypical concepts first, followed by variations.
- Present concepts, principles, and rules to supplement rote learning of facts.
- Make material more meaningful by relating it to real-world problems.

Because schemas differ among cultures, instruction and training products should be designed to begin at a schematic level common to both the trainer and the participants. From that point, the instruction should help participants learn at an enhanced level by providing elaborative associations, advanced

FIGURE 4–6
Instructional Products

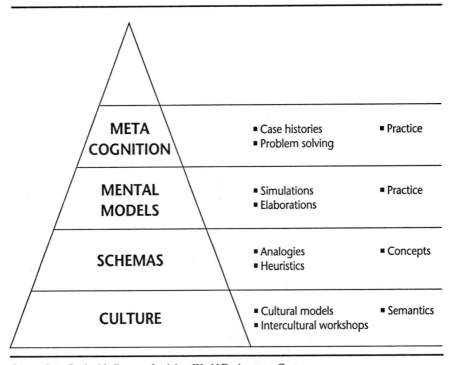

Source: Peter Beckschi, director of training, World Environment Center.

organizers, topical headings, and the use of mnemonic devices (e.g. acronyms and visual imagery). The total set of individuals' schemata reflects their culturally conditioned view of reality.

When designing instructional products, specific cultural schemas need to be incorporated in order to make a transition in knowledge. When teaching industrial safety, the impact on the group of employees at the plant may need to be emphasized over the individual—particularly in collective cultures. Also, the need to wear certain items of personal protective equipment may go unheeded unless the entire plant workforce is included. In many locations, shoes—let alone safety shoes—are not worn. Making transitions from existing schemas to target schemas requires careful task analysis. The research and application studies from knowledge engineering in this area are promising.

MENTAL MODELS

Mental models are an individual's conceptualization of task demands, methods for accomplishing the task, and how the domain involved works. A domain is an individual's knowledge about a specific job or subject area. Mental models are evolving entities that an individual uses to interpret environmental events (episodes) and to decide how to respond to them. Researchers have found that in learning problem-solving skills, the majority of errors can be traced to improper or faulty mental models.

In "Foundations in Learning Research," R. M. Gagne and R. Glaser identify four tactics for encouraging the use of mental models in learning and performance.[9] The first tactic involves discovering models of everyday situations that people bring to a training situation and refining them as part of the training process. Second, a task analysis can identify the development of models as an individual progresses from novice to expert. This same sequencing also can be used in instruction. Third, trainers can explicitly teach "good" mental models of the task. The fourth tactic involves taking advantage of models currently used by trainers to guide and improve their performance by providing examples and counter examples and situations in which to apply and test their models. Generally speaking, the success in training airline pilots from around the world is attributable to high-quality mental models using a variety of instructional products.

Whenever a model is presented as part of the training, it should clearly and succinctly represent the task characteristics and constraints. Its format varies depending on the domain and its cultural representations, which may include stories, graphics, maps, and flowcharts.

METACOGNITION

In addition to basic mental operations, individuals have the ability to monitor and control their conscious cognitive processes. This ability, called metacognition, implies that people can learn to optimize their cognitive processes. Metacognitive skill is an important factor affecting performance, and many recent studies that have directly taught such skills to learners have produced very encouraging results.[10] Perhaps one of the most important findings to emerge from this research is that these heuristics and thinking skills must be explicitly taught to be effective.[11] Incorporating explicit instructions in learning and problem-solving strategies and methods for monitoring skill development and allocating cognitive resources can increase motivation for trainees and reduce overall training time.

DESIGNING INSTRUCTION FOR COGNITIVE DEVELOPMENT

The major implication for the transfer of skills and abilities from one cultural context to another is its suitability for the audience. Usually, but certainly not always, training should be subjected to the rigors of a well-thought-out, well-planned, and well-designed program. Depending on the nature of the material to be learned, different designs have proven to be more effective than others.[12] What is most important is that a repertoire of design products is available for the trainer to alter or modify the training program to fit the new audience.

In "Internalizing Instructional Design," Barbara Martin suggests that instructional designers select, adapt, develop, and refine a wide variety of instructional products. These products can be placed on a continuum from tightly organized to loosely structured ones (see Figure 4–7).[13] The products that are tightly organized usually follow a highly articulated model such as ISD. These products are used extensively in training for high-risk operations such as civil and military aviation and power plants and are suitable for high-power distance cultures. Those on the other side of the continuum provide a supporting framework that lets the designer or trainer adapt products to fit a specific situation. For training programs to be successful in different cultural settings, a variety of training products along the continuum are necessary.

For example, case studies or role plays must be culturally appropriate. Videos that portray office settings or interpersonal situations in America may be irrelevant. By offering a variety of products and techniques, designers can help trainers overcome barriers to effective delivery worldwide. By using cultural models from Hofstede and specific country information, training products can be developed or adapted as appropriate for a specific culture.

How training is approached separates the expert from the novice trainer. Expert trainers, particularly those effective in working with diverse ethnic/cultural groups, possess a rich repertoire of models and theories that transcend the usual five-phase ISD model. According to Glenn E. Snelbecker, an eclectic Differentiated Instructional Systems Design (DISD) is the most appropriate approach since it copes with models, theories, and innovations from cognitive science and other sources that are likely to be successful in developing a training program.[14]

The DISD model (Figure 4–8) depicts a structured modular and flexible design approach. The overall main instructional plan (identified as MIP) addresses the complete program consisting of component instructional plans

FIGURE 4–7
A Continuum of Instructional Products

• Highly structured	• Highly flexible
• Replicable means and ends	• Replicable outcomes
• Format allows wide dissemination	• Potential exists to be disseminated and used by others with modifications
• Useable as produced	

Source: Barbara Martin, "Internalizing Instructional Design," *Educational Technology*, 24 (May 1984).

(CIPs) prepared for delivery. The CIPs are further reduced to sub-components (SCIP) and sub-sub-components (SSCIP). In addition, a RIP (recurring instructional plan) serves as a computer shell for recurring instructional sequences that differ primarily in terms of the content rather than in the structure of the instructional unit. For example, a RIP can be based on certain research-based or culture-based procedures that apply to the main instructional plan.

Each of the components of the DISD model possesses two features of note:

1. Each provides some aspects of instruction independently.

2. Each has an interdependent relationship with the other units.

Collectively, the units fulfill the training requirements. What the DISD approach offers is a means of incorporating existing design features that can be altered or modified for a new audience. For example, if a training program in the United States calls for individual responses for demonstration of outcomes, but group responses are more appropriate for the collective cultures, the DISD approach allows for flexibility in meeting audience needs.

COMPETENCIES FOR TRAINING DESIGNERS

According to Martin, at least 10 competencies are needed for designers and trainers. These are modified to reflect recent field experience in training abroad.[15] The designers and trainers need to:

FIGURE 4–8
The Differentiated Instructional Systems Design

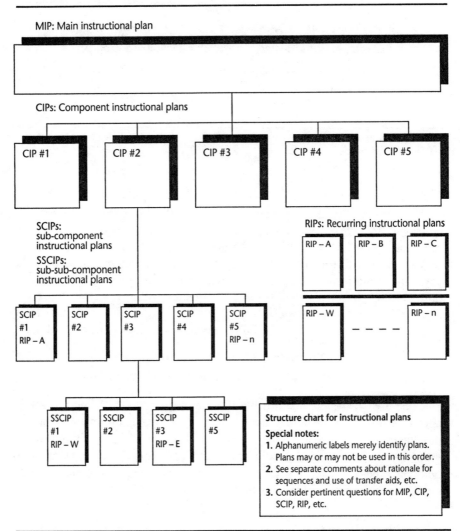

MIP: Main instructional plan

CIPs: Component instructional plans

CIP #1   CIP #2   CIP #3   CIP #4   CIP #5

SCIPs:
sub-component
instructional plans

RIPs: Recurring instructional plans

RIP – A   RIP – B   RIP – C

SSCIPs:
sub-sub-component
instructional plans

| SCIP #1 RIP – A | SCIP #2 | SCIP #3 | SCIP #4 | SCIP #5 RIP – n |

RIP – W   RIP – n

| SSCIP #1 RIP – W | SSCIP #2 | SSCIP #3 RIP – E | SSCIP #5 |

Structure chart for instructional plans

Special notes:
1. Alphanumeric labels merely identify plans. Plans may or may not be used in this order.
2. See separate comments about rationale for sequences and use of transfer aids, etc.
3. Consider pertinent questions for MIP, CIP, SCIP, RIP, etc.

Source: Glenn E. Snelbecker, "Practical Ways for Using Theories and Innovations to Improve Training," in George Piskurich, ed., *The ASTD Handbook of Instructional Technology*, ASTD and McGraw-Hill, 1992.

1. Determine the scope of the project with information from the host culture.

2. Conduct a needs assessment, including an analysis of the resources, culture, schemas, and potential implementation procedures.

3. Assess trainee and group performance characteristics.

4. Conduct content, task, or job analyses.

5. Use and integrate research from various sources.

6. Write objectives and performance criteria.

7. Sequence learning outcomes.

8. Select, adapt, or produce culturally relevant learning strategies.

9. Produce a variety of instructional products.

10. Design culturally acceptable procedures for evaluating the design, products, and outcomes.

DESIGN CONCLUSIONS

The technology, institutions, and other interrelationships that draw us together in globalization are increasing. Unfortunately, our knowledge of the human side of globalization has not kept pace with these developments. Only recently has research and application of new techniques from cognitive science been able to improve instructional design and its products for intercultural applications.

There is no easy prescription to improve the performance of global trainers. The designers and trainers must become more sensitive to different cultures while keeping abreast of recent developments in intercultural training, cognitive science, learning theory, and instructional design.

Most cultures will permit trainers to attempt more productive and innovative training scenarios if the participants are asked to help design the instruction to meet their cultural as well as learning needs. No design can provide for all the cultural nuances. However, if trainers introduce more metacognitive skills for understanding different cultures and internalizing instructional design, host nationals can then share in the overall design of global training.

While instructional design practices in the United States have produced outstanding training results in this country, cross-cultural training design presents new challenges. These challenges require designers to be more knowledgeable about design methodologies that are more suitable for the design of cross-cultural training. In addition, designers need to be sensitive to the cultural differences between trainers and trainees.

The chapter discusses culture as a group's collective intellectual environment and includes both those elements of culture—such as literature, games, religion, and cooking—that are in our conscious awareness and those elements—such as the tempo of work, courtship practices, conception of beauty, and conception of cleanliness—that are not in our conscious awareness.

Because language is the most conspicuous expression of a culture, trainers are encouraged to learn at least a few key phrases. Conducting training in another culture is a serious venture and requires early preparation and qualified translators or trainers who are native speakers. Because body language differs from culture to culture, trainers and designers must be knowledgeable about the physical cues they receive and give and their meanings to the cultures in which they train.

Training design and presentation recommendations include:

1. Provide opportunities for trainees to apply the material to their own cultural situation.

2. Be empathetic to feedback from trainees.

3. Look for opportunities to take advantage of cultural differences.

4. Be sensitive to a culture's methods of learning and working.

5. Learn about the local region and its technology.

6. Remember that, as outsiders, the trainer and designer should try to understand and discuss gaps in understanding.

The role of an instructional designer is to relate and modify the learners' ideas, concepts, and beliefs to new information and knowledge. When developing cross-cultural training, the designer should capitalize on characteristics that are shared among cultures. Hofstede provides continuums in five categories that help trainers and designers understand the characteristics they hold in common and those that are different from the countries in which they will train.

Understanding thought processes can help trainers improve their ability to comprehend other cultures. Four elements of memory (metacognition, mental models, schemas, and culture) and the instructional products or methods that can be used with each to bridge cultural differences are provided.

Training should be structured to promote optimal schema development. Trainers should:

- Relate new information to existing knowledge schemas.
- Organize material following its conceptual structure.
- Teach prototypical concepts first followed by variations.
- Present concepts, principles, and rules to supplement rote learning of facts.
- Make material more meaningful and related to real-world problems.

Since mental models are an individual's conceptualization of task demands, trainers should:

- Discover models of everyday situations.
- Conduct a task analysis to identify model development as an individual goes from novice to expert.
- Teach good mental models of a task.
- Take advantage of models currently used by trainers and improve them by adding examples and applications.

Metacognition implies that people can learn to optimize their cognitive processes. Training should include explicit instruction in learning and problem-solving strategies and methods for monitoring skill development.[16]

A wide variety of instructional products are important to use for cross-cultural training. Additionally, research shows that designers and trainers should possess at least nine competencies.

Chapter Five

Developing a Global Training Curriculum

There are many roads to truth and no culture has a corner on the path or is better equipped than others to search for it.

— G. T. Hall
Beyond Culture

W hether corporations like it or not, they are competing globally," says John Garrison, manager of recruitment and development for Colgate-Palmolive in New York.[1] To support the multinational company, the training curriculum must reflect this globalization. Many international corporations are presenting some form of global management training—most often for managers who are transferred on international assignments.[2]

The global business environment demands employees who can work effectively across national and cultural boundaries or can, in author Kenichi Ohmae's words, manage "in a borderless world."[3] Cross-cultural training gets high marks for helping individuals adjust to an assignment in another country and for improving task performance, according to a study by J. Stewart Black of Dartmouth's Amos Tuck School of Business and Mark Mendenhall of the University of Tennessee's School of Business Administration in Chattanooga.[4] Examining a number of studies on the effectiveness of cross-cultural training, they found general agreement that this training is an important tool for successful expatriate assignments.

Here are some of the outcomes training can produce for companies conducting business in a global environment:

- Improve ability to identify viable business opportunities.
- Avoid wasting resources on ill-conceived ventures.
- Give a competitive edge over other global players.
- Improve job satisfaction and retention of overseas staff.
- Prevent lost business due to insensitivity to cultural norms.
- Improve effectiveness in varying business environments.

The secret of effective, cost-efficient, cross-cultural training lies in targeting training effectively to the person and the job responsibility.

Cross-cultural training is often described in terms of differing interpersonal behaviors. For example, Americans are said to be very direct in approach, specifically expressing what they want, while the Japanese are described as being much more circumspect. However, Hal B. Gregersen and Black have identified underlying traits for success in global settings.[5] While some of these traits may not be changed by training, they can be used as considerations in choosing personnel for global assignments. Some positive traits for global effectiveness are:

- Lack of ethnocentrism.
- Sociability—the desire to meet and be with people.
- Interest in communicating.
- Ability to substitute host-country food, customs, etc., for home-country ones (sushi for hot dogs, for example) and the degree to which the person enjoys this.
- Nonauthoritarian leadership style.
- A negotiating rather than controlling style of conflict resolution.

At the Tuck School, Black and his colleagues have identified five areas of key cross-cultural differences where doing business abroad is likely to be very different in kind or degree:[6]

- Monetary systems in which the relative values of currencies fluctuate (and with them wages, profits, and other financial areas they influence).
- Legal systems that vary not only in particulars but in underlying assumptions.
- Political structures that differ in operation and in how they influence and are influenced by business.

- Market and market structures that require subtle changes in products and marketing techniques from country to country.

Additionally, the balance of control between corporate headquarters and the local company is a problem in itself. Cross-cultural training for corporate executives may be of a general nature, making executives aware of the issues present in global dealings, or it can be country-specific. Language is also an important skill in this area.

Cross-cultural skills include differences of communication and style. Some of them may be considered soft skills. Failure to understand appropriate and courteous behavior in another country, however, has doomed or endangered many endeavors. American executives will not pick up such skills in the U.S. education system, in their normal life experiences, or in their business career. So corporations must provide this training.

How can a training director effectively plan a multinational training program? In developing this global training process, we have discussed the preliminary steps in earlier chapters:

- Assessing the company's global training needs.
- Assisting management in thinking globally.
- Developing a global training strategy.
- Designing company guidelines for multinational training.

Now it is time to decide what courses can provide the training employees need to successfully conduct business in all parts of the world. In this chapter a menu of various global training programs currently offered is arranged by categories: cultural awareness, multicultural communication, country-specific training, executive development, language courses, and host-country workforce training. Also some of the content of these courses—and even the workshops themselves—may at times be repetitive. However, this listing provides valuable information in creating courses for multicultural training.

CATEGORY 1—CULTURAL AWARENESS

The first curriculum category, cultural awareness, is an introductory course in working with people from other countries. Most training in this category consists of understanding how culture affects work relationships and how understanding these differences can promote teamwork and productivity within an organization. Reviewing the following courses in cultural awareness can provide insight into what topics can be included in this type of global training.

Global Interface Skills Training

For global interface personnel, Moran, Stahl &Boyer International (MS&B International) designs and conducts custom-tailored training programs that promote the awareness needed for recognizing the specific cross-cultural interface issues that these people confront and the communication and interpersonal relations skills appropriate to their individual situations. These programs may focus on a single country, a geographical region or selected specific countries, or on general intercultural relations techniques.[7]

Going Global

One of the first steps in global training is increasing employees' multicultural awareness. If this were a college course, it would accurately be called Global 101. International Training Associates of Princeton (ITAP), an international consulting firm, states that the purpose of its Going Global course is to provide managers and support employees with facts, analyses, and a forum to review their own roles in contributing to the successful globalization of the company.[8] This one-day program will:

- Present the company's global mission using a company videotape.
- Highlight changes in markets that require changes in business.
- Present the segment "understanding world-class competition."
- Stress effective management approaches and diverse workforce environments.
- Help each employee examine his or her role in light of global market changes.
- Examine corporate and individual citizenship in a world of new markets and prospects.

Going Global is available for groups of up to 100. Its premise is that, while top management may be aware of the relationship between the new markets and requirements for the workforce, this information often has not reached those who could bring about the change.

Going Global provides:

- Information about the company's international strategic plans.
- An analysis of international markets and corporations.
- An opportunity for employees to develop the necessary knowledge and awareness about global business so that they, in turn, can provide increased contributions to their company's international competitiveness.

Employees who understand the nature of international markets and international competition will be more productive and capable in the global corporation.

Doing Business Internationally

Having the ability to manage and do business with people from different parts of the world is no longer a nice-to-have skill; it is a necessity. The urgency in the business community to find and develop individuals who can be successful at the international level is not just another fad—it is a question of economic survival.

Doing Business Internationally: The Cross-Cultural Challenges, designed by Training Management Corporation, is a foundation course for building the skills needed to operate successfully in a wide variety of cultural settings and meeting the international management challenge.[9] The two-day seminar sharpens the skills critical to functioning effectively in unfamiliar business environments as well as learning about significant global trends and major cultural regions. Course content includes:

Day One

> *Module 1.* Global Business Thinking
>
> *Primary Objective.* Analyze key global trends and their impact on current business practices.
>
> *Units.* A. Going global: changes in the marketplace.
>   B. Key global players.
>   C. Doing business in new ways.

Module 2. Cross-Cultural Awareness

Primary Objective. Recognize the impact of cultural differences on business relationships.

Units. A. The impact of diversity.
B. Culture simulation.
C. What is culture?
D. Developing cultural effectiveness.

Day Two

Module 3. Cross-Cultural Communication

Primary Objective. Identify and overcome intercultural communication barriers to achieve greater synergy.

Units. A. Doing things differently.
B. Communication process.
C. Handling cross-cultural differences.
D. Marketing and sales.

Module 4. Working across Cultures

Primary Objective. Adapt key business skills to maximize effectiveness when working across different cultures.

Units. A. Culture and management.
B. Adapting management skills.
C. The success factors of international managers.

Cultural Awareness

Trans Cultural Services presents an introductory workshop on Cultural Awareness.[10]

The course outline includes:

- Culture—what is it?
- Cultural variables.
- The cultures we live in.
- What's American about the "American"? The tie that binds us.
- The issues of culture and diversity for the manager.

The theory of management is universal, but its implementation varies from culture to culture. In the culturally diverse workforce, perceptions and understanding of the roles and responsibilities of the manager, supervisor, and employee vary widely.

This course is designed for managers, supervisors, and other professionals who wish to enhance those skills necessary for working successfully with and in other cultures.

Participants will:

- Develop an awareness of cultural variations in management concepts and styles and recognize the relationship between management style and effective intercultural interactions.
- Identify those situations in which differences in style and expectation may create misunderstandings that interfere with productivity and effectiveness.
- Anticipate potential difficulties that may arise for the manager of the culturally diverse workforce and devise strategies for recognizing, minimizing, or eliminating problems arising from cultural miscommunications.
- Develop a plan focusing new knowledge to improve intercultural communications at all levels of interaction.

Perspectives: An Experience in Bridging Cultures

DeVaney-Wong International provides An Experience in Bridging Cultures, a workshop on international perspectives.[11] Believing that there is no one methodology or formula for helping people develop a multicultural perspective, the company adapts this workshop to the special needs of the customer. The workshop outline includes:

- A new vision of the world.
- Getting to know you—what you bring.
- Fun facts—practice with dos and taboos.

- Unlocking the keys.
- The global community—gaining a multicultural perspective.
- Planning to learn.

Cultural Awareness Program

INSERV offers a one-day cultural awareness training program.[12] The outline includes:

- American values and assumptions: competency exercise (beginning).
- Introduction to cross-cultural assumptions and values, Part I: communication issues.
- Introduction to cross-cultural assumptions and values, Part II: identity issues.
- Competency exercise (continued).
- The bureaucracy simulation.
- Individual and group evaluation of the simulation.
- Practical applications.

Global Perspective

Lawton International presents Global Perspective seminars on properly interacting, verbally or nonverbally, with international clients—which can mean the difference between obtaining or losing an important account.[13] Encouraging international companies to conduct business with your company requires a working knowledge of international business practices.

Incorporating international business etiquette within management training is crucial to a company's profitable bottom line. Executive Etiquette for Global Transactions: A Global Perspective prepares managers for conducting business successfully in the world marketplace. This seminar provides an introductory global overview of many countries, including Germany, Japan, Mexico, Russia, and Saudi Arabia.

Global 101 is an excellent and necessary foundation for a company's global training curriculum. A training program that ends there, however, is not enough. A university student majoring in business does not complete Business 101 and immediately move into the job market with a well-rounded business education degree. The introductory course is a beginning, a starting point from which to launch more specific information and skill development.

Cross-Cultural Technology Transfer

MS&B International offers a course on cross-cultural technology transfer—
the primary task of many personnel abroad.[14] What are the consequences and
costs if the transfer is not effective? Experience has shown that consequences can range from frustration, anxiety, resentment, ill will, inefficiency,
and substandard performance to the total failure of a project.

It is not enough to transfer hardware or manufacturing operations, maintenance, and safety procedures to another country. Personnel receiving the technology must learn how to use the hardware and to carry out the procedures
effectively. This requires formal classroom training as well as on-the-job training. Personnel with the necessary technical qualifications—who have had no
cross-cultural preparation or training—are often assigned the task of passing
on their knowledge to counterparts. Mere possession of technical qualifications does not guarantee the skills required for effective training. Training in
the methods and techniques of transferring technology is just as important.

Because even experienced trainers may not actually have trained counterparts from a different culture, these trainers cannot foresee problems they
might encounter. It is essential that trainers understand the cultural differences that create barriers to technological transfer and to learn ways of getting through these barriers. In MS&B International's programs, participants
learn how cultural values affect technology and the technical learning
process, and they also practice the skills required for performing their jobs in
the country of assignment.

CATEGORY 2—
MULTICULTURAL COMMUNICATION

Multicultural communication is another category in global training. Although
all cross-cultural training increases the ability to communicate transnationally,
it is often important to offer curriculum courses specifically focused on communication between cultures. This training can be presented for employees
from any country. Although this category is not language training, special
consideration is focused on the varying degrees of language capabilities.

Communication Skills for Foreign-Born Professionals

Intercultural Development, Inc. provides language training in fluency, oral
presentation skills, and basic pronunciation for professional employees who
have a high degree of English proficiency but need further work.[15]

Communication Strategies for Non-Native Speakers of English

A workshop by International Orientation Resources (IOR) enhances the participants' abilities to communicate with non-native speakers of English.[16] It is recommended for all the company employees who have frequent international contact, either on the telephone or in person. Subjects addressed by the workshop include:

- Using internal business communication techniques.
- Organizing content and limiting complex information.
- Using core language and simple speech patterns.
- Checking for lack of comprehension.
- Avoiding lose-face situations.
- Recognizing the complexities of the English language.
- Evaluating the non-native speaker's capacity to speak English.
- Understanding difficulties faced by non-native speakers.

Language and Culture of American Business

Global Interact presents a training program on Language and Culture of American Business.[17] This seminar outline includes:

- Background to American culture.
- Coping with cultural differences.
- U.S. business etiquette.
- Interacting with American business associates in social settings.
- Body language in American business.
- Manners of written business English.

Intercultural Communication

Priscila C. Montana & Associates presents a seminar on cultural awareness and diversity in the workplace.[18] This program on intercultural communication includes:

- Dynamics of change and transition.
- Cultural awareness and diversity—definitions and significance.

- Valuing multiculturalism.
- Culture-specific information.
- Differences, similarities, and impact of cultural, verbal, and nonverbal communication styles.
- Developing and maintaining cultural synergy.

International Protocol and Presentation

Success in today's global economy requires an understanding of how business is conducted internationally. Yet the ways of doing business differ across cultures. An unpolished presentation is bad business, and a breach of etiquette can result in loss of business. A one-day program presented by Pachter and Associates focuses on the correct way to handle people with tact and diplomacy—whether they are from Paris, Tokyo, or Cairo.[19]

The objectives of the program are:

- Boost your confidence about doing business internationally.
- Learn ways to increase your cultural awareness.
- Understand the importance of etiquette in international business.
- Communicate successfully with people from different countries.

Outline:
  I. Greetings and introductions in different countries.
  II. Communication signals across cultures.
      A. Language.
          1. When English is the common language and when it isn't.
          2. Using an interpreter.
      B. Nonverbal communication.
          1. Dress.
          2. Gestures.
          3. Eye contact.
          4. Space and touch.
  III. Ways to make an effective presentation overseas.
      A. Delivery techniques.
      B. Use of visual aids.
  IV. Conducting business.
      A. In the office.
          1. Timing.

    2. Use of technology.

    3. Written communication.

  B. Out of the office.

    1. Entertaining and dining customs.

    2. Gift giving.

Working with International Visitors or New Citizens

Survival skills necessary for people from other cultures to live and work successfully in the United States, adjust to the American culture and business environment, and deal with immediate needs, are presented in this Intercultural Development, Inc., program.[20]

Foreign National Program

This three-day program is presented by INSERV for employees from other cultures who will be working in the United States and/or their spouses.[21] Content topics are:

Day One

- Introduction to the United States.
- Historical themes shaping American society.
- Concepts shaping American society and culture.
- Living in the United States.

Day Two

- Equal rights in America.
- Business etiquette.
- Leadership and authority in the U.S. corporate environment.
- Decision making and problem solving in the U.S. corporate environment.
- The training process in America.
- The expatriate family.

Day Three

- Intercultural communications: barriers to communication.
- Intercultural communications: conflict resolution.

- Being effective in the United States.
- Adjustment and culture shock.
- Someday you'll come home again.

Cross-Cultural Training and Orientation

This program presented by Bennett Associates on cross-cultural training and orientation is for expatriates and third-country nationals.[22] The course goal is to develop each participant's knowledge, awareness, and skills that ensure their effectiveness, productivity, and comfort during an overseas assignment. The program includes Bennett Associates' core process and:

- Cross-cultural business skills for managing the assignment.
- Intercultural communication effectiveness.
- Planning for a successful international assignment.
- Frameworks for understanding cultural differences.
- Practical approaches to culture shock management and lifestyle adjustment.
- International transition and stress management.
- Strategies for becoming an effective international manager.
- Daily life in the host country: business practices, social customs, and expectations.
- Special issues: spouses and families abroad.
- Area studies, history, geography, politics, economics.
- Repatriation as a pre-departure issue.

International Teambuilding

Global Dynamics, Inc. provides a session on international teambuilding that describes and demonstrates a system for creating high-performance learning teams where the staff works with or comes from diverse cultures.[23] These work teams learn to adapt quickly in today's dynamic and competitive business environment through personal mastery, appreciation of differences, team learning, shared visioning, and systems thinking (adapted from *The Fifth Discipline—The Art and Practice of the Learning Organization* by Peter Senge and the Myers-Briggs Type Indicator I).[24]

Workshop participants learn how to:

- Assess their problem-solving styles to gain insight into their own styles and the styles of others.
- Apply their knowledge about problem-solving styles to improve working relationships with people from other cultures.
- Recognize how their implicit cultural assumptions affect their interactions in international settings.
- Identify specific situations where misunderstandings are likely to occur when working on an international team.
- Assess their behavior in conflict situations and apply this knowledge to international situations.
- Develop responsive strategies and an action plan that will be implemented through peer coaching.

Cross-Cultural Teamwork

A two-day workshop, Cross-Cultural Teamwork by Training Management Corporation, explores cross-cultural, organizational, and interpersonal barriers to effective teamwork and task performance.[25] Participants gain valuable training in the skills needed to build and participate in multicultural teams.

Course Content Outline:

- Module 1—The Importance of Culture
  How we perceive those who operate according to different cultural values and norms, sources of cross-cultural misunderstandings, and key aspects of culture.
- Module 2—The Role of Values in Business Interactions
  Values clarification, how to understand and work with people with different cultural values, and how values are reflected in business behaviors and customs.
- Module 3—Goal Setting
  Stages in goal setting, difference between goals and objectives, characteristics of effective goals and objectives, strategic versus operational goals, and goal setting as a leadership tool.
- Module 4—The Organization as a System
  Establishing purpose, targeting planning, identifying the interrelationships between the corporate business units, organizing a performance model, and performing impact analysis.

- Module 5—Teambuilding
  Definition of a team, characteristics of effective and ineffective teams, achieving synergy, team development states, effective listening techniques, and managing meetings.
- Module 6—Conflict Management and Negotiation
  Conflict management styles, steps to conflict resolution, and a model for cross-cultural negotiations.
- Module 7 - Personality Issues
  Work personality differences, resolving conflict caused by personality differences, and management implications.
- Module 8—Leadership and Management (for executives)
  Definition and assessment of management and leadership behaviors.
- Module 9—Employee Appraisals, Development, and Empowerment (for executives)
  Feedback and appraisals, methods to develop employee skills, and participative management skills.

Training Workshop for Companies
Acquired by the Parent Company

Managing newly acquired companies will be more productive if managers understand American business culture, as well as the company's corporate culture. IOR presents a workshop that assesses foreign companies acquired by the company and educates their managers to allow them to more easily integrate into the company corporate structure.[26] The workshop addresses the company corporate culture, as well as American business and management styles.

Workshop topics include:

- Analysis of significant elements of the company's corporate culture that will affect the acquired company.
- Advantages to be gained through the company ownership.
- Defining areas of potential challenges for the two entities and devising proactive strategies and solutions.
- A comparison of American and local national business environments: priorities, values, and styles.
- American communication styles.
- American decision making and negotiations.

- Coping with structural change.
- Effective intercontinental communications, including how to communicate (in person, phone, fax, video, or writing), how often to communicate, and whom to communicate with.
- How to work in a multinational team.
- Defining a chain of command.

Joint Venturing in Japan

A seminar on joint venturing in Japan is offered by Global Dynamics, Inc.[27] The course includes:

- Cultural aspects of doing business in Japan.
- Briefing on Japan.
- Understanding strategic alliances.
- Joint ventures, mergers, and acquisitions.
- Strategy development.

The Intercultural Passport

The Center for international training and education (Cite) has developed the Intercultural Passport Seminar, based on the research findings of the world's leading authority on national cultures, Professor Geert Hofstede of the University of Limburg, Masstricht, The Netherlands.[28]

Hofstede's research, based on a six-year IBM survey of more than 100,000 respondents, identified common workplace problems but different solutions among different nationalities. These variations of behavior and attitudes in IBM managers and employees could be explained only by differences in national cultures.

While Hofstede identified four dimensions among IBM entities, a group of his colleagues in China identified a fifth dimension unique to Asian cultures. Combining their work, they created the Five Dimensional Model of National Cultures. The 5-D Model portrays these differences as:

1. Structure and power—The ways cultures create power and authority structures.
2. Individuality and community—The role of personal identity and integration within groups.

3. Tasks and relationships—The preference for caring about relationships or caring about tasks and results.

4. Uncertainty avoidance—The degree of tolerance of ambiguity.

5. Confucian dynamism—The pragmatic values that dominate the East explain the long-term challenges facing businesses that seek to penetrate Asian markets.

Cite associates have used Hofstede's research to develop an intercultural education program for executives and managers from multinational corporations or domestic businesses seeking to successfully enter the global marketplace.

Increasing Overseas Business Effectiveness

This program in problem solving in overseas business negotiation and communication through increasing knowledge of other countries and understanding cultural differences is offered by Intercultural Development, Inc.[29]

Managerial Mediation

Meeting the challenges of a global economy and the increasing trend toward workforce diversity requires insight into the influence of culture on the behavior, thoughts, and communication styles of varying intercultural and intracultural groups and individuals. "Successful international businesses are led by those who develop the necessary skills of communicating and negotiating across cultural barriers," says Sally Normand McReynolds who provides training in these areas.[30]

Business Basics for the Foreign Executive

Global Interact offers a seminar in business basics for the foreign executive.[31] This training course includes:

- Negotiating cross-culturally.
- Interacting with U.S. clients in business settings.
- Making presentations.
- Participating at meetings.
- Writing for American business.
- Telephoning skills.

International Sales Skills

Global Dynamics, Inc. provides this international sales skills seminar for account executives, managers, and others who market products to clients whose culture is different from their own.[32]

In this training program, participants examine critical issues for selling in the global marketplace: advertising, prospecting, initial qualifying, positioning organization and products, making appointments and contacts, opening the sales call, diagnosing and probing, presenting, handling objects, closing, followup and delivery/installation, expanding the account, customer service, account strategy planning, nature of sales, selection of sales personnel, client relationships, sales protocol, nature of persuasion, basis of trust, risk-taking propensity, distribution systems, importance of international trade shows, terms of agreement, the sales cycle, values and beliefs, authority/decision making, nonverbal behavior, language, communication, and contract and legal implications.

Global Dynamics, Inc. also has designed a seminar on international trade shows. This session helps participants develop individual and corporate strategies for effective performance at international trade shows. By looking at how successful organizations make the most of international trade shows, participants explore how strategies between domestic and international trade shows differ.

CATEGORY 3— COUNTRY-SPECIFIC TRAINING

Preparing an expatriate manager for an assignment outside the United States was one of the first categories of global training developed. Companies quickly recognized that the success of the transfer depended on the expatriate's knowledge and understanding of the host country's culture. Second, it also became apparent that the spouse and family members needed to be prepared for the culture shock as they learned to adapt to the new culture. The third phase of country-specific training was recognized in more recent years. The shock suffered by the employee upon returning to the United States was often dramatic, especially as the speed of corporate change accelerated. Countering the Rip-van-Winkle experience became a major factor in maximizing the global experience for the individual and for the corporation. Many courses are currently offered to increase the success of the expatriate experience.

Employees sent on short-term assignments need country-specific training as well. The content of the training may need to be more focused and topic-specific than for those headed for multiyear assignments, but it is still necessary. Sending someone to France to look into business opportunities or to work through the details of a joint venture requires cross-cultural knowledge and skills.

Pre-Departure Orientation

Smooth family adjustment to, and return from, an assignment abroad enhances expatriate productivity, performance, and morale.

MS&B International's individualized and highly interactive training programs are designed for the entire family so that positive attitudes are reinforced at the earliest point.[33] These are not off-the-shelf curricula; rather, they are programs tailored to the concerns and interests of individual expatriate families. The program provides the basic training and information needed to facilitate the transfer of employees and their families to other countries. Special components on leadership and management, as well as technology transfer to counterparts of other cultures, are included when appropriate. The program fosters positive attitudes that promote continued learning and adjustment. The MS&B International approach is also valid for employees transferring from their home countries to the United States or to other countries.

Living and Working Outside the United States

Intercultural Development, Inc. offers training for American business personnel and families to live overseas, understand other cultures, learn strategies and skills to cope with the new environment, and avoid early returns to the United States.[34] An example of these country-specific workshops is their program on living and working in Spain.

The overall goal of this workshop is to increase individual awareness of the effect of Spanish cultural practices in business and to improve the effectiveness of a company that is dealing with Spanish people. Much has been written about doing business with the Japanese and other countries but little attention has been focused on Spain. General topics such as decision making, negotiating, and social behavior are covered in the workshop. The workshop also offers participants an opportunity to explore specific issues in which their companies are directly involved.

Two prerequisites to learning another culture are to first acknowledge and understand one's own culture and, second, to form an attitude of avoiding value judgments. These topics are emphasized in the workshop. Americans must be willing to extend themselves by learning more about the Spanish culture and the way the Spanish conduct business.

Global Orientation Programs

ITAP's Orientation Programs are available for company transferees and their families relocating for a substantial period of time outside their home countries. These programs are provided for Americans going overseas and for international employees entering the United States.[35]

The purpose of ITAP's Orientation Programs is to improve, through training, the quality of life of relocating employees and their families, thereby increasing their productivity and retention rates in their new locations.

Relocation services—such as introducing global employees to a local area, providing information about schools for employees' children, and assistance in finding housing—can also be provided.

ITAP's Orientation Programs include:

- A modular training approach based on a needs assessment.
- Lifestyle planning segments.
- Special programs for children.
- Experiential sessions in the community for international employees.
- Key informants from the relocation country.
- An introduction to housing, schooling, and related support services.
- Dual-career programs for spouses.

Family Adjustment to an Overseas Assignment

Numerous overseas business assignments have failed because of adjustment difficulties faced by family members who accompany a businessperson on a long-term overseas assignment. The everyday stresses of living and working overseas can be extremely debilitating.

A Global Dynamics, Inc. program helps families understand the process of cross-cultural adjustment to their new host country.[36] A family is helped to identify the particular needs of each individual. Each family member develops strategies for successful overseas adjustment. A focus on business procedures and protocol in the new culture enhances the effectiveness of the employee while a concentration on everyday living benefits all family members.

Equipped with a more realistic understanding of the new culture and the process of adjustment, the family is then prepared to take full advantage of the opportunities for personal growth that can come from an overseas assignment.

Business Familiarization Program

INSERV, a Dallas-based international consulting firm, provides training for Americans living and working in other countries.[37] An example of these two-day programs is seen in the following outline of their Business Familiarization Program for Argentina.

Day One

- Introduction to the Argentine Republic.
- Historical themes shaping Argentine culture.
- Concepts shaping Argentine society and culture.
- Intercultural workplace issues: Argentine corporate style.
- Intercultural workplace issues: business interactions and business etiquette.

Day Two

- Intercultural communications: barriers to communication.
- Intercultural communications: conflict resolution.
- Negotiating with Argentine companies and employees.
- Being effective in Argentina.

Doing Business Globally

Global Dynamics, Inc. presents a two-day course in strategies for success for doing business in specific countries.[38] An example of this is provided in its workshop on doing business with Japan. This course is for executives, managers, and professionals who conduct business with the Japanese, as well as those who host Japanese people, those who deal with them by telephone or mail, those who have indirect contact (i.e., product design), and those whose responsibilities affect international operations with Japan through planning, staffing, or training.

Course objectives include how to:

- Learn Japanese business and social protocol.
- Learn how historical and social factors affect Japanese business.
- Examine how cultural differences between Japanese and Americans affect business relationships.
- Gain valuable hands-on insights for improved performance from veterans.
- Examine the link between international business operations and globalization strategy.
- Develop a strategic action plan for working with the Japanese.

Culture-Specific Training: China

George Renwick offers consulting and culture-specific design and training for corporations that are transporting employees across borders.[39] An example of his programs is one he provides for Northeastern China. This training includes:

1. Establishing base camp.
   a. Getting acquainted.
   b. Setting the stage.
   c. Confirming objectives.
   d. Exploring participants' own culture and values.
   e. Speaking Mandarin.
2. Becoming acquainted with the terrain.
   a. Living each day in Shenyang, China.
   b. Exploring your new neighborhood, discovering China.
   c. Recognizing cultural differences (and similarities) that can make a difference.
3. Face to face: the major challenge.
   a. Communicating with confidence.
   b. Interacting effectively with Chinese: pitfalls, possibilities, practice, and more practice.
4. Making a meaningful life as a foreigner.
   a. Fulfilling special responsibilities, pursuing special opportunities in China.
   b. Adjusting successfully, contributing significantly.
   c. Planning encouraging entrance strategies that will work.
   d. Creating your foreign community.
5. Connecting, reviewing, confirming.

Returning Employees

Following their return to the United States, expatriate families may encounter problems in making the adjustment to life back home. Few corporations involved in international operations provide adequate support to employees and their families to help them readjust to living in the United States after they have completed an assignment abroad. The problems result not only in the reduced effectiveness of returning employees but also in an alarming rise in the attrition rate of these employees a short time after their return. In many instances, this is because employees returning home are often dissatisfied with their new assignment and are resentful toward their company. Since the corporation more than likely valued these employees highly enough to have selected them for the assignment in the first place, their leaving the company is quite costly. Thus, the firm has lost a sizable investment.

MS&B International helps participants in these programs examine adjustment problems and ways of dealing with these problems.[40] The participants become aware of changes that have occurred in their company, their country, themselves, and their families during their assignment abroad. During their readjustment period, they anticipate, and make provisions for, the personal and professional impact of these changes.

Reentry Programs

ITAP's reentry programs have two segments: Returning to Live at Home for employees and their families, and Returning to Work at Home for employees.[41] Because expectations are high, reentry is often more difficult than the initial overseas move for both families and employees. Special issues for children (such as changes in schooling), for spouses (such as returning to careers), and for employees (in terms of workplace reintegration) are explored.

These reentry programs may be provided for Americans returning from abroad or for international employees returning to their home countries from stays in the United States. Lifestyle planning techniques help family members reconnect their living, working, and leisure patterns to their home turf.

For the returning employee, an assessment is made of changes in managerial style. Work reentry strategies are discussed. When appropriate, ITAP will work with the client's career development specialist to assist during the reentry period.

ITAP's reentry programs provide ways:

- For families to assess their international experience.
- For employees to examine changes in work habits and competencies.
- For providing career counseling.
- For children to examine ways in which they have changed and what to anticipate in their new schools.

Reentry programs are essential for globalizing corporations to retain experienced international executives. Retention of skilled employees is *much* less expensive than their replacement and, for the company, provides continuity and appropriate succession possibilities for top-management positions.

Expatriate Reentry

Clarke Consulting Group, Inc., tailors a reentry program to the needs of individuals and their families who are being reassigned to their home country.[42] Program length is normally two to four days. The company offers Japan-based training for Americans and other expatriates who are returning home and for Japanese expatriates who have returned to Japan. It also offers U.S.-based training for Japanese and other expatriates who are returning home and for American expatriates who have returned to the United States. This program is most effective for expatriates just prior to departure for and up to six months after their arrival in their home country.

Objectives of the course are for participants to:

- Reflect upon and assess their experience abroad.
- Increase their knowledge of the process of reentry and understand where they are in that process.
- Determine the effects of changes in their value systems and patterns of behavior on intrafamily and extrafamily relationships.
- Affirm the need of family members for each other and affirm how as a family they can best readjust.
- Identify ways to use the knowledge and skills learned abroad in social and work situations in their home country.
- Develop strategies for moving forward in the process of readjustment and identify realistic goals for managing that process.

The program also:

- Facilitates the employee making a smoother transition to and more effective start in his or her own position.
- Reduces the anxiety and stress that accompany readjustment, thereby reducing time and energy loss during the process.
- Promotes better communication between family members.
- Facilitates adjustment to unexpected changes in oneself, in others, and in one's environment.
- Promotes maintenance of a healthy balance between a focus on self and a focus on others during the readjustment process.

Working Internationally

Every businessperson who works or anticipates working in the international marketplace must contend with the serious and very costly mistakes and misunderstandings caused by differences in business practices and social customs.

Global Dynamics, Inc. provides a seminar designed to enhance the effectiveness of all persons whose work brings them into contact with people from other countries.[43] Anyone who conducts business abroad—as well as those who host people from foreign cultures or who deal with them by telephone, fax, or mail or whose responsibilities affect international operations— needs to understand how cultural differences in social customs and business practices can and do affect individual and group performance. In this seminar participants learn the important skills necessary for success in the global marketplace. Participants learn:

- Cultural dos and taboos of international business practices.
- Major differences in doing business around the world.
- How to use case studies of actual international business activities to improve performance.
- How to adapt to the different negotiation styles around the world.
- How to adjust to an international assignment and develop appropriate coping strategies.
- What situations are most likely to cause problems when working internationally.
- Which traits and skills are necessary for individual and corporate cross-cultural effectiveness.
- International business and social protocol.

- How to use nonverbal messages to increase effectiveness.
- How to develop a strategic action plan for improved international business operations.

International Briefings

ITAP's International Briefings are designed for short-term, frequent business travelers and teams working on specific international business objectives.[44] International Briefings are constructed as two- or three-day programs using related modules. Each briefing is conducted somewhat differently, depending on the business purpose of the group in training. This determines the particular mix of modules used. A sample program follows:

Day One. The first day provides participants with a general background of the target country or region, including political, economic, social, and cultural factors. Participants are introduced to these subjects in short 20-minute segments, after which they form small groups for the purpose of relating the information acquired to their business purposes. Over lunch, a film or video is shown which illustrates a significant aspect of the business purpose and the country. Afternoon sessions focus more specifically on the business objective. For example, a group looking at a pharmaceutical acquisition would be briefed during this period on the competitive climate for pharmaceuticals in the country and region, the major players, and key factors in financing, marketing, etc.

Day Two. Specialized programs are introduced here. A two-day negotiation session will begin at this time, if the business purpose involves negotiations. For these groups working closely with nationals from the target country, an international one-day teambuilding segment is introduced. For those managers who will be spending significant periods of time in the country at an affiliate or other host company, day two will focus on international management assessment and training.

Regional/Country Business Briefings

This series by Training Management Corporation provides participants with the cross-cultural skills they need to do business effectively with members of selected countries and regions.[45] Country briefings are provided in a two-day format and include, but are not limited to: Germany, Italy, France,

Russia, Japan, Canada, and Mexico. Regional briefings include, but are not limited to, the Caribbean, Latin America, Asia, Middle East/Africa, and Europe.

Each briefing presents an in-depth analysis of the country or region under study, conveys practical information and facts for doing business, fosters understanding of the significant differences between the country or region and the United States, identifies the business styles and approaches most effective with members of the given culture(s), and facilitates strategy development for improved cross-cultural business relationships in general. The content includes:

- Module 1—Overview of the Country or Region
  Geography, history, politics, religion, government, ecomonics, business trends, social structure, sources of national pride, and relations with the United States.

- Module 2—The Importance of Culture
  Cultural perception: how we perceive those who operate according to different cultural values and norms.

- Module 3—The Cultural Gap Between Americans and Members of the Country or Region
  Cultural differences in attitudes toward key aspects of management and national/business values.

- Module 4—Information for Doing Business
  Establishing contacts, correspondence tips, language considerations, use of interpreters, image enhancers/taboos, entering into a contract, and sources of help.

- Module 5—Business and Social Customs
  Greetings, dining and entertaining, gift giving, etiquette, topics of conversation, dress, use of business cards and titles, and meeting behaviors

- Module 6—Strategy Development
  Application of program concepts and skills through completing the personal development contract.

Business Briefings and Seminars

Bennett Associates works in collaboration with corporate leaders who must manage the increasingly challenging task of working globally to develop relevant, value-added programs.[46] The company's business briefings and seminars integrate state-of-the-art intercultural education and training models, including:

- Updating key managers on significant business, political, and economic trends of major global regions (Europe, Middle East, Pacific Rim, Africa, Pan America).
- European Community '92 briefing for companies positioning themselves for the single-market Europe.
- Country-specific briefings for executive travelers to increase their professional and social effectiveness with foreign employees, clients, agents, and suppliers.
- Cross-cultural negotiations.
- Planning and problem-solving techniques for multicultural teams.

Intercultural Business Programs

Unrecognized cross-cultural differences can affect the success of international negotiations, marketing and sales efforts, and ongoing business relations. MS&B International offers training programs designed to improve the effectiveness of home-based staff needing to travel or to communicate regularly with clients and associates abroad.[47] These programs improve business effectiveness by promoting an understanding of cultural influences, by teaching specific country business and management practices, and by helping interpret the behavior of business people from other cultures. The result is enhanced business and social communication, and increased credibility in conducting business interactions abroad and with counterparts/business partners in the United States.

Working with the Japanese

Clarke Consulting Group, Inc. has various seminars on working with countries in the Pacific Rim, especially Japan:[48]

- Working with Japanese program for people who travel to Japan periodically.
- Japan-bound training program preparing American managers for extended assignments in Japan.
- For the Japanese on working with Americans.
- International management development program, an intensive immersion training program designed for Japanese managers of Japanese companies on special start-up assignments with their subsidiaries or of American companies on training and development assignments at U.S. headquarters.

- Binational organizational development is to key American and Japanese corporate executives focusing on the organizational development of the binational corporation.
- Corporate culture analysis and report—offers research and consulting to American and Japanese joint-venture partners and to binational organizations in a home office-subsidiary relationship focusing on analysis of the corporate culture of the organization.
- The technology transfer facilitation program is a two- to three-week program designed for small groups of engineers and trainers who deliver technical training to non-native English speakers.

Living and Working in Japan

This cross-cultural training program for Americans is designed by East-West Consultants to quickly prepare American business people for overseas assignments in this increasingly important country and culture.[49] Although Japanese and American cultures are used in this sample overview, the course can be successfully adapted to meet the needs of participants from any two cultures. Specific content with regard to background, need, and areas of concentration would vary; approach, format, and methodology would remain basically the same.

Program Objectives. As a result of the workshop, participants will be better able to:

1. Understand that their concepts of what's important in business (and in life) are culturally based and not universally shared.
2. Recognize the key areas in business where Japanese and American cultural priorities and beliefs differ.
3. Apply verbal and nonverbal communication skills in job-related, cross-cultural communications.
4. Identify typical areas of cultural misunderstanding such as:
   - Directness.
   - Willingness to commit.
   - Trust.
   - People versus task orientation.
   - Authority and power structures.
   - Role of tradition and respect.
   - Time orientation.
   - Profit and other motivations.
5. Understand and respond to Japanese business practices, protocol, and management styles.

6. Develop action plans designed to enhance cross-cultural communication and management skills.

The areas of concentration include:

1. Overview of cross-cultural training.

2. Successful intercultural adjustment.

3. Culture: definition, components, characteristics.

4. Cultural self-awareness.

5. The role of perception.

6. Factors creating and influencing cultural environment:
   - Religion.
   - Education.
   - Economics.
   - Politics.
   - Family.
   - Class structure.
   - Language.
   - History.
   - Natural resources.
   - Geography.

7. The American world view: beliefs, values, norms, attitudes, assumptions, expectations.

8. The Japanese world view compared and contrasted with the American.

9. Comparison of key elements of Japanese and American cultures:
   - Sense of self.
   - Norms and values.
   - Dress and appearance.
   - Relationships.
   - Mental processes and. learning styles.
   - Notions of time.
   - Communications and language.
   - Food and eating habits.
   - Beliefs and attitudes.
   - Work habits and practices.

10. The Japanese business context:
    - Relationship to nation and the world.
    - Professional behavior.
    - Social behavior in business situations.
    - Corporate organization.

11. Doing business with the Japanese.

12. Strengths/weaknesses of each system.

13. Japanese business etiquette.

14. Establishing working/interpersonal relationships.

15. Flash points in Japanese/American business interactions.

16. Debriefing and participant evaluation of program.

CATEGORY 4—EXECUTIVE DEVELOPMENT

"If you develop a product in your market, you have to be thinking if this will play in Korea. It's understanding the linkages between countries," says John Fulkerson, vice president of organization and management development for Pepsi-Cola International in Somers, New York.[50] Smart companies recognize this, he adds, and are trying to fill their executive ranks with managers who have international experience. There are many types of seminars for executive global development, including specific global management training, teambuilding, specific country workshops, and global briefings to help executives track global events and processes that directly affect the company, its products, and markets.

Global Business Briefings

IOR sees the benefits of its global business briefing workshops as training senior managers to:[51]

- Acquire greater knowledge of key global business centers.
- Increase intercultural effectiveness.
- Access expert international resources.

The expatriate curriculum includes several programs:
1. Expatriate selection assistance.
   a. Selection of more effective and better-informed expatriates.
   b. Reduced risk of costly failed assignments.
2. Pre-departure cross-cultural training.
   a. Increase understanding of the destination city and culture.
   b. Identify and build upon intercultural skills.
   c. Clarify the family's transition issues.
   d. Enhance strategies for goal setting and role changes.
   e. Become more effective in the international assignment.
3. On-site assistance.
   a. Dramatically eases cultural transition stress.
   b. Relieves the employee of a myriad of essential settling-in details.
   c. Gives immediate answers to pressing questions/concerns.
   d. Ensures ongoing support for the spouse.
4. Expatriation assistance.
   a. Retain valuable employees after repatriation.
   b. Learn techniques for using new international skills.

Global Briefs and Roundtables

The WORLD Group realizes that today's business environment of accelerating global change and competition means executives need a regular flow of relevant, strategic information.[52] It holds sessions for senior executives that ensure familiarity with global social, economic, and political trends, as well as an understanding of global business opportunities. Strategic and organizational issues related to global integration can also be explored with external experts.

Topics for these briefings and roundtables include:

- High-growth strategies for the Pacific Rim.
- Global leadership and the high-tech corporation.
- Competing in the new Europe: beyond 1992.
- Industry assessments for the Soviet Republic and Eastern Europe.
- *Maquiladoras* in Mexico.
- Effective niche strategies in Japan.
- Post-war prospects in the Middle East.
- Japanese automotive in the United Kingdom.

The WORLD Group also offers world-class training in: cross-cultural skills, international negotiating, global technology development, global marketing, world-class customer service, foreign languages, and global finance.

The Effective Global Manager

Managing in a borderless, multicultural business landscape presents both unprecedented opportunities and professional challenges. Training Management Corporation's two-day program on the effective global manager is ideally suited for the organization wishing to train its managers to be successful leaders in the global arena.[53] Participants gain the knowledge and skills required to put top management's strategic plans into effect for penetrating and operating in global markets. Fostering global thought patterns and broadening cultural perspectives is a primary objective of the program.

In this course, participants will:

- Learn the distinctions between international, multinational, and global companies.
- Discuss the key forms of a global organization and the implications for management.

- Examine the role of culture in business and the management implications of working with those who operate according to different cultural values and norms.
- Identify U.S. cultural assumptions and values, examine how they are reflected in management practices, and contrast these with the values of key countries
- Apply cultural insights to management communication across national and organizational lines.
- Explore organizational techniques for cross-cultural implementation.
- Practice and apply techniques for multicultural team management.
- Learn key management skills in a global context, including leadership, planning, organizing, project management, decision making, problem solving, performance appraisal, motivation, and employee development.
- Gain skills practice in analyzing and solving cross-cultural and organizational problems through case studies that simulate real-life situations.

International Executive Seminars

ITAP's seminars are interactive briefings that bring the new realities of the international marketplace directly to executives with international concerns and responsibilities.[54] Introduced by ITAP, they were co-developed by Eric Kruger, an international strategist and economist with extensive experience in advising senior and middle-level executives on the rapidly changing international environment.

The seminars are presented at corporate offices or at off-site management retreats or sales conferences, where they can serve as an event for stimulating discussion and strategic rethinking.

Four kinds of seminars are offered:

- Executive seminars on the international environment.
- Executive update briefings: the international outlook.
- Briefings on critical international issues.
- Executive briefings on selected regions and countries.

The typical executive seminar starts with an up-to-date perspective of major recent and upcoming changes in the global environment. It focuses on the forces driving change in today's key economies and traces their cause-effect interrelationships around the globe on those aspects of the business environment that the executive must deal with. Unlike the usual economic presentation, these briefings also address changes in the political and financial market arenas, and come out with a clear conclusion as to how they too are likely to affect crucial factors, such as interest and exchange rates and the pace of economic activity and trade.

Recent briefings have drawn executives' attention to:

- The coming global shortage of capital.
- The impact of changes in Germany on world interest rates.
- The new world system linking exchange rates.
- International price trends on U.S. competitiveness.
- New trading patterns affecting U.S. markets abroad.

The final spotlight is on the industry and market in which the executive will be working with emphasis upon the bottom line: the risk/profit outlook.

Global Project Team Management

Global Project Team Management seminars by Training Management Corporation focus on the role of the international project manager and the skills necessary to accomplish this role in the ever-widening global business environment.[55] The content of this three-day course includes:

Module 1—The International Project Manager's Role

- Characteristics of a global corporation and implications for the project manager.
- State of the global competitive environment.
- Responsibilities of the project manager along the life cycle.
- Project scope and charter.
- Measures of project performance: efficiency, effectiveness, and adaptability.

Module 2—Project Planning and Organizing Tools

- Project scheduling tools: Gantt charts, milestone lines, and CPM/PERT.
- Organizational issues for the global corporation.
- Project planning process blueprint: task-responsibility matrix, project organization chart, schedule and work breakdown structure.

Module 3—Project Monitoring and Control

- Design and use of a project information system.
- Project control techniques: scope and resource control, time and cost control, and earned value analysis.
- Action (re)planning: identifying project jeopardy and decision making.

Module 4—Global Leadership Skills

- Models for understanding cultural differences in business values, management styles, and organizational cultures.
- Cross-cultural communications model.
- Building multicultural project teams.
- Life cycle of a project team.
- Participative planning and decision making.
- Setting goals and measures for project teams.
- The global project manager as a change agent.
- Motivating multicultural teams.
- Subordinate analysis and employee development.
- Understanding the conflict process: diagnosis-assessment and selection of conflict resolution strategies.
- Project meeting behaviors and skills.
- Situational leadership styles.
- Effective delegation.
- Business/social customs and management practices of the key world regions.

Module 5—Case Studies, Instruments, Demonstration Problems, and Personal Development Contract

Programs for International Assignees to the United States

International assignees to the United States have problems adjusting to life and work that are similar to those of North Americans assigned abroad. These problems can be particularly severe for the employees' spouses, whose English language ability tends to be limited and who do not have the opportunity to adapt to the language and culture in a work setting.

MS&B International provides cross-cultural training and relocation assistance to international assignees and their families who will be living anywhere in the United States.[56] The unique approach combines a formal training program with the hands-on assistance of a professional relocation counselor. The training program is similar to that for North Americans assigned abroad. It focuses on the knowledge, attitudes, and skills required to adapt to the North American culture and to live and work effectively as expatriates in the United States. The relocation counselor builds on this training by providing an accompanied tour and specific information on the local area. This is followed by assistance in finding a home.

Multicultural Management and Teambuilding

Differences in employees' cultural backgrounds may be hidden sources of misunderstanding, friction, and conflict. Employees or trainees assigned to the United States, ethnic minorities in the workforce, and bicultural joint-venture project teams are a few of the personnel for which multicultural teambuilding is necessary.

MS&B International designs and conducts custom-tailored workshops and seminars that help employees understand their own and their counterparts' culturally determined management styles—and learn specific skills and techniques for functioning effectively within a synergistic management team. These programs promote intercultural awareness, acceptance, and mutual respect among co-workers of diverse backgrounds.

CATEGORY 5—LANGUAGE COURSES

Language Training

Business success in markets abroad often depends on effective communication in another language. MS&B International conducts training programs in more than 35 languages, delivered by more than 100 certified instructors. Instruction is determined by the learner's needs, not by the requirements of a predetermined curriculum or textbook. Course content is not only job- or role-specific, it is also cost effective.

Each course can be delivered at the client's location. Expatriates and their families can also participate in the company's state-of-the-art integrated language and cross-cultural programs.

Language Programs

In IOR language programs, the participants learn through a variety of methods:[57]

- Listening to a native speaker.
- Functional role play.
- Reinforcement drills.
- Use of audiovisual materials.
- Interactive language/culture exercises.

Language Tutoring Services

LinguaCall International, Inc., provides various language services.[58] The firm consists of more than 70 language specialists (translators, interpreters, typists, proofreaders, editors, instructors, and teachers) available to serve any aspect of second-language needs. The company's services include:

- Instruction programs: private phone lessons to office or home for all languages and for all levels of proficiency.
- Translation service: specializing in document translation and/or type-setting into Japanese, French, Spanish, German, Russian, and Chinese. Includes brochures, business cards, facsimiles, letters, and manuals.
- Interpretation service: to help clients with phone calls, business meetings, and overseas visitors. Available for all languages.
- Tailored conversational group instruction programs: up to five persons per group on location for all languages and for all levels of proficiency.
- Tailored private conversational instruction programs: on location for all languages and for all levels of proficiency.
- Cross-cultural training: to attune American businesspersons to cultural differences and to better prepare them for more effective business dealings and negotiations.
- General consulting on language-related needs: includes developing language instruction programs, training programs, consulting, and coordinating translation projects.

CATEGORY 6—HOST-COUNTRY WORKFORCE TRAINING

A global training area that has received little attention is preparing the host-country employees for the transfer of expatriate managers. Charles M. Vance of Loyola Marymount University's College of Business Administration has conducted research on training the host-country workforce for working with expatriates.[59] He believes the success of the expatriate management assignment depends on many factors in addition to just preparing the expatriate manager. Those "on the other side of the coin" in the host country may be able to contribute significantly to productivity during the assignment through appropriate preparation and training. The past neglect of host-country preparation supports the rather ethnocentric belief that the success of the expatriate assignment depends almost totally upon the expatriate manager and family.

Host-country workforce training should involve cultural awareness of the expatriate's own culture, especially in areas where past experiences have led to culture conflict. The training should also include how to avoid these problems or how to deal with them should they occur. The focus of training for the host-country workers should encompass:

- What kinds of behavior the workers can expect.
- Why the expatriate manager may behave in an unpredictable, unconventional, and often unacceptable way from the host-country culture point of view.
- How to cope effectively with cultural differences.

Vance argues that the multinational company has a moral responsibility to provide preparation for the host-country workforce as well. Such duties can include:

- Helping all employees complete their assignments successfully.
- Avoiding the semblance of discriminating treatment.
- Encouraging complete integration into a global economy.
- Fostering personal enlightenment and enrichment.
- Helping individuals develop useful, marketable skills.
- Contributing to the development of a larger and more skilled national labor force.
- Encouraging a long-term focus on creating a lasting value for stakeholders rather than on a short-term profit for only a few.

Two studies that Vance conducted also support the need for host-country workforce training.[60] One was based on information obtained from interviews with Mexican personnel directors and managers in *Maquiladora* operations of U.S., Japanese, and Korean multinational corporations. Vance's findings represent a framework for strategic human resource planning where effective host-country workforce training can lead to increased performance of the international operation and also the expatriate management assignment, as well as the building of a more effective global orientation for the parent corporation. In a comparative analysis of host-country national training in five countries of the Pacific Rim, Vance found that the key to success for the transnational firm is its ability to train and develop the host-country nationals—at all levels—in such areas as corporate mission, strategy, management skills, and specific business expertise and practice.

GLOBAL TRAINING METHODS AND SELECTION CRITERIA

In addition to reviewing the categories of international training courses, methodology and the selection process is also important in designing a global training program. Black and Mendenhall in "A Practical but Theory-Based Framework for Selecting Cross-Cultural Training Methods," examined the effectiveness of cross-cultural training relative to three outcomes: cross-cultural skill development, cross-cultural adjustment, and job performance.[61] They found that:

- Of the 10 studies that examined the relationship between cross-cultural training and self-confidence concerning one's ability to function effectively in cross-cultural situations, nine found a positive relationship.
- Nineteen out of 19 studies found a positive relationship between cross-cultural training and increased cross-cultural relational skills.
- Sixteen out of 16 studies found a positive relationship between cross-cultural training and cross-cultural adjustment.
- Eleven out of 15 studies found a positive relationship between cross-cultural training and job performance in the cross-cultural situation.

Figure 5–1 presents several fundamental cross-cultural training methodologies that trainers can use.

FIGURE 5–1
*Fundamental Cross-Cultural Training Methodologies**

Information or fact-oriented training: Trainees are presented via lectures, videotapes, and reading materials with various facts about the country in which they are about to live.

Attribution training: The attribution approach focuses on explanations of behavior from the point of view of the native. The goal is to learn the cognitive standards by which the host-nationals process behavioral input so that the trainee can understand why the host-nationals behave as they do and adapt his or her own behavior to match the standards of behavior in the host country.

Cultural awareness training: The aim is to study the values, attitudes, and behaviors that are common in one's own culture, so that the trainee better understands how culture affects his or her own behavior. Once this is understood, it is assumed that he or she can better understand how culture affects human behavior in other countries.

Cognitive-behavior modification: The focus here is to help trainees link what they find to be rewarding and punishing in their own subcultures (work, family, religion, etc.), and then to examine the reward/punishment structure in the host culture. Through an examination of the differences and similarities, strategies are developed to help trainees obtain rewards—and avoid punishments—in the host culture.

Experimental learning: The goal of this approach is to involve the trainees as active participants, to introduce the nature of life in another culture by actively experiencing that culture via field trips, complex role plays, and cultural simulations.

Interaction training: Here trainees interact with natives or returned expatriates to become more comfortable with host-nationals and to learn from the first-hand experience of the returned expatriates. The methods can range from in-depth role-playing to casual, informal discussions.

*Adapted from Landis and Brislin (1983)

Source: J. Stewart Black and Mark Mendenhall, A "Practical But Theory-Based Framework for Selecting Cross-Cultural Training Methods," *Human Resource Management*, Winter 1989. Reprinted by permission from John Wiley & Sons, Inc.

Mendenhall and Gary Oddou's framework for selecting training methods acknowledges that the degree of expected interaction and similarity between the native and host cultures is important in determining the cross-cultural training method.[62]

Symbolic and Participative Modeling in Training

Within social learning theory there are basically two modeling processes: symbolic and participative.[63]

- Symbolic modeling simply involves observing modeled behaviors. However, this observation can have two forms. The first form consists of the trainee hearing about the behavior and then translating those verbal messages into imagined images. Examples of cross-cultural training methods that exhibit this modeling process include verbal factual briefings, lectures, and books. The second form of symbolic modeling involves the participant actually seeing the behavior being modeled. In this case, the trainee both sees and retains an image of the behavior and is more cognitively involved. Specific methods that generally exhibit this type of modeling include films, role modeling, demonstrations, and nonparticipative language training.

- Participative modeling adds participation of the trainee to modeling the behavior. Participation can take the form of verbal participation when the trainee participates and models the behavior by describing verbally what can be done. Global training methods that exhibit this type of participative modeling include case studies and culture assimilators. The second form of participative modeling involves more physical participation such as role plays, interactive language training, field trips, and simulations. Trainees are more cognitively involved when they also physically participate in modeling the behaviors being taught.

There are also two basic forms of practice or rehearsal that increase the level of cognitive involvement during symbolic or participative modeling. Cognitive rehearsal involves the mental rehearsal or practice of the modeled behavior (for example, practicing eating with chopsticks in one's mind), and behavioral rehearsal involves actual physical practice of the modeled behavior.

CASE STUDIES

Let's look at examples of the type of global training curriculum used in three corporations. These three case studies are from Intel Corporation, Eastman Kodak, and Procter & Gamble.

Intel Corporation

Intel, a high-technology firm, has manufacturing and sales offices in worldwide locations. Each major site has a training organization with a training manager from the local country. As Intel has engaged in greater multinational partnerships, one of its major thrusts has been to increase the quality of relationships and the exchange of information and training technology. Once each year a week-long international training summit meeting is held. The purpose of this meeting is to decide on a corporate-wide training strategy for the year, as well as to promote communications and the building of relationships among the training organizations around the world.

Because its engineering and manufacturing talent spans geographies and nationalities, Intel is a highly culturally diverse company both worldwide and within the United States. In 1983, Intel launched its intercultural training program with the development of multicultural integration classes for foreign-born professionals. Based on the success of these classes and the growing awareness of global competence, Sharon Richards was selected as intercultural training manager—and for the first time a position solely focused on intercultural training was created.[64]

Intel's intercutural training program has five components:

1. *Intercultural Awareness.* "The main objective of intercultural training is the development of cross-cultural awareness," states Richards. Intercultural training for first-line supervisors, mid-level managers, and senior managers is integrated with management topics and business objectives. "Our goal is to incorporate cross-cultural education into all training. For example, if a course on how to conduct effective meetings is taught, one needs to address how culture impacts meeting processes and procedures." It is impossible to work in a global company without interfacing with people of many different cultures. So, teaching managers—and all Intel employees—to be culturally aware and sensitive is the first step in intercultural training. While culture-specific information and lists of dos and don'ts are important, worldwide expertise is unrealistic.

   Managers cannot always be trained in the culture of each of the employees they manage, particularly if they have multiple cultures in their work group. Thus, they must learn what it means to manage various cultures and develop their ability to know when they need to seek additional culturally-specific information or help. "Even employees' expectations of their manager are different in different cultures. Some countries expect the manager to know how to perform every step of the jobs they supervise. Other cultures see managers as those who provide the tools necessary for their groups to be productive and perform well. So, intercultural awareness is the foundation level of all of our training," Richards continues. "We want to extend and expand our managers' competencies in culture as well as business areas. In today's global competitive environment, a successful manager or executive must have a global mentality and intercultural skills."

2. *Multicultural Integration Program.* This series of classes developed for foreign-born professionals focuses on communication skill building and career development. Classes offered include accent improvement, effective oral presentations, speaking under pressure, technical and business writing, American idioms and vocabulary in the workplace, and American business culture. In the multicultural integration workshop, managers who were born and raised in other countries and have been successful within the company are used as role-model presenters. They discuss their own careers and speak of career planning and professional growth and development. Additionally, the workshop offers an informal environment for individual questions and networking.

3. *Culture Specific Training.* This training focuses on working and doing business in or with people from different cultures. Training for interfacing with other cultures includes the countries of Japan, Israel, the Philippines, Malaysia, Ireland, Korea, and Taiwan. Not only do employees learn about the cultures of these countries during the courses, but they also examine their own individual culture. They then learn how to bridge the communication gap and work successfully together.

4. *Training for International Assignments.* Competing in a global environment necessitates worldwide cross-training and business interface, particularly with the increasing numbers of joint ventures and business partnerships. Managers and their families going on international assignments are provided language and country-specific orientation and education prior to departure. This training is usually presented by an external consultant with extensive experience living and working in that country and culture.

5. *Intact Team Training.* This level of training is designed to support specific corporate business initiatives. When Intel forms a joint venture with a non-U.S. company, training for team members is imperative for the success of that venture. The role that corporate cultural differences as well as national cultural differences play is often underestimated. Intel is increasingly incorporating intercultural perspectives into teambuilding. As an example, in one situation when engineers from Japan were brought to the United States for training, an external consultant who is fluent in Japanese was available to work with the employees and their families during their stay. The consultant assisted with translation and English language training. During meetings the consultant acted as a liaison and clarified information in one-on-one situations. The consultant was also available for family emergencies such as interfacing with hospital personnel or taking the family to the doctor. This intercultural support helped the work team to get off to a fast start and facilitated by easing both employee and family adjustment to a culturally different lifestyle.

Richards emphasizes the importance in selecting consultants who provide culture-specific training. "The criteria should not only be that they are from that country and know the language and culture, but they should also be versed in current business practices. They must be able to apply intercultural theory and training to business situations, needs, and applications. Corporate intercultural training must go beyond the surface culture of food, dress, and language to provide the deeper understanding of individual awareness—how we operate and communicate from our own culture—and how all cultures can best work together."

Intel primarily uses external consultants for its intercultural training. It also leverages its internal expertise by selecting international employees from its workforce to present words of wisdom and communicate as role models in its training sessions. Whenever possible, employees from the focus culture are included in classes to share their perspectives, and increasingly managers are coteaching with consultants to provide bicultural training teams.

One of the major trends Richards has noticed in the last year is the increased level of intercultural awareness among Intel managers. "Their willingness and commitment to international training is growing." And within the training organization itself, whenever a new training course is discussed, designers seek cultural input upfront so the course can be effective for all employees worldwide. "Managers must develop a repertoire of skills and must become aware that there is not just *one* way of operating in a multicultural environment. There may be a preferred way of communication, but individuals do not have to give up their primary cultural values to communicate effectively."

Richards believes that it is often easier to recognize the need for cultural training when the culture is very different from your own culture. When differences are more subtle—as between Ireland and the United States—questions arise about the need for training. Anyone in the intercultural training arena hears the debate over emphasis in training on cultural similarities versus cultural differences. Richards points out that the similarities do not get us into trouble in other cultures, but differences can cause major problems. "Anyone working in a global workforce must also realize that, unfortunately, no matter how much intercultural training and experience you have had, you will at some time make a cultural error. How you handle the situation, and what you do about it to take the sting out of the words or behavior, is extremely important," Richards states.

Global training for the multinational corporation must be real-time business training. In fact, it is just-in-time training. For Richards it is difficult to plan what international programs Intel will need six months from now. Change happens fast. Decisions are made quickly. "We in human resources cannot anticipate just what our company's next business venture will be. An executive walks in and says that we have just signed a joint-venture agreement and need to send 20 employees to a specific country within a few weeks. This may be a national culture which is not included in our training program. The training manager must be flexible enough to know that the best ways of developing and presenting that program may not be possible because of the time constraints. You must be flexible and able to implement what you need when you need it. This is a major challenge in supporting the company's intercultural training needs. But it is both an incredible challenge and opportunity," Richards concludes.

Eastman Kodak Company

Eastman Kodak Company has been a multinatonal corporation for more than 90 years with marketing houses and manufacturing plants in some 140 international locations. The corporation has a reputation for being committed to the development of employees through many avenues, one of which has been a large investment in training. Currently, regional marketing offices and major manufacturing plants comprise a total employee population of approximately 133,000. Each region and major plant has responsibility for the training and development of its managers. They generally link local development planning to regional training resources located in each regional headquarters. Most of the training organizations are self-sufficient, but are free to draw on corporate management education as well as imaging training resources in Rochester, New York, the headquarters city.

Up to now, Kodak has not had a "standard, worldwide human resource plan, but a decentralized, customized approach has been our strategy," says Mary Anne Williams, corporate director of executive education.[65] Cross-cultural training has been provided as needed, in most cases to individuals or units that were conducting business in another country or were planning to locate abroad. This training has ranged from language learning to total cultural/business immersion training for expatriates and their families.

For the past six years, corporate education has provided a five-segment program, "International Business Operations," that includes a substantial amount of time spent on cross-cultural awareness and skills. This program is targeted at professionals and managers who are in the early stages of interacting with non-U.S. operations and customers.

"With increasing emphasis on globalization in all three Kodak sectors (Imaging, Health, and Chemicals), we are seeing an increase in the number of international/cross-cultural learning initiatives," Williams states. "For example, the Chemicals Group is currently committing a significant amount of time to cross-cultural training for its entire management team. This team of approximately 50 managers attended a five-day program focusing on countries in the Asia-Pacific region. Additionally, it will be launching study trips to selected countries in Asia for in-depth learning focused on strategic issues."

The corporate group of Kodak executives, representing all three sector presidents, their leadership teams, and corporate staff executive vice presidents, have been led by Eastman Kodak Chairman Kay R. Whitmore to engage in management conferences of two-to-three-day duration focusing on dimensions of globalization. Faculty for these conferences has come from the United States (i.e., University of Michigan, MIT, Harvard University) as well as non-U.S. (i.e., INSEAD, Stockholm School of Economics). Whitmore is also sponsoring six executive forums on Japan, bringing in world-renowned speakers to further develop global mindsets among the senior leadership group. Study trips will also likely follow these forums. "In the case of corporately sponsored events like management conferences and executive forums, the design originated from within Kodak, and the delivery is by worldwide faculty. All of the events are work/action oriented, not lecture or strictly case-based learning," Williams explains.

Corporate executive education also runs a two and one-half week corporate program for high-potential middle managers from all three sectors. The focus here is to broaden their knowledge and skills as general managers, with a decidedly *global* tone. For every one of these Kodak management programs held in the United States, two will be held in a non-U.S. location (Europe, Asia) to take advantage of international political-economic developments, faculties, and business speakers. "The most recent management program in 1992 was held in Brussels, and a heavy emphasis was placed on issues and opportunities emerging from the formation of the EEC," says Williams. "For such programs, we bring in senior Kodak executives as speakers, exposing participants to both corporate and regional strategies and cross-cultural issues, and reinforcing a vision of our global firm."

Whether providing training to individual expatriates and operating teams or providing a support to a long-haul cultural change process, Williams' advice is about the same: "Start where your customers' needs start. Identify what practical issues are on their minds and satisfy those needs with action-oriented learning. It won't be long before longer range cultural issues present themselves, and the customer will desire to learn more about the culture, customs, language, even the strategic mind of the country or region. Beginning with the seeming esoteric information can be a big turnoff, unless the customer buys into and really understands the value of total immersion techniques. Normally, we find them turned off by too much too soon. A sensitive needs analysis up front is absolutely essential. The second most important factor is to think of this kind of learning as a progressive journey, not one-time training," Williams advises.

Procter & Gamble (P&G)

Another example of multinational training is Procter & Gamble. P&G has subsidiaries in 50 countries around the world. Thirty of these are manufacturing sites, and the other locations house advertising, financial, and sales personnel. Prior to 1979 the company was using the early 1970s model—adopted by many corporations—of transferring employees from the United States to international subsidiaries. These U.S. employees managed the site and trained the local employees in parallel work. When local employees became proficient in their jobs, the U.S. employees turned the operations over to them and returned to the United States. American managers were selected for international assignments on the basis of technical competence and availability. The ability to persuade others that this assignment would be best for the company as well as the manager was also a major factor. This model is no longer used. The corporation found it is more efficient to train local employees in the technology as they manage their own site.

In 1979 P&G initiated strategic planning for a major technology transfer to Japan. With the assistance of external consultants, it developed a three-pronged approach to multicultural training:

1. Language learning opportunities were provided to U.S. employees in learning the Japanese language and also to the Japanese in learning English.
2. Cross-cultural training was presented for employees in both Japan and the United States.
3. All employees were given training in P&G's corporate culture to provide a common base of operations.

This leading-edge approach, while time and labor intensive, proved a major factor in the success of the company's Japanese operations.

In 1992, out of an employee population of 100,000, P&G has approximately 1,000 third-country nationals (expatriates). Fifty percent of these expatriates are from the United States and 50 percent are from international locations working outside their countries. Ten percent of this international employee group have been brought to the United States and are serving as inpatriates at American sites. Most of P&G's standard training curriculum is adopted worldwide. The local training staff adapts the courses and presents them locally.

"So often, human resource professionals want a checklist of global training issues and it just doesn't work that way," says Mike Copeland, international training and development manager.[66] "International company needs are in continual flux, and employees in a multicultural environment are also adapting and changing," Copeland explains. "As companies become more global and employees spend more time working in other cultures, the lines between the cultures become less distinct. If you are training someone from Europe on how to do business with Americans, do you present the cultural nuances of New York, California, Minnesota, or Texas? Even American culture differs according to region."

Copeland believes that one of the critical issues of multicultural training is that results data is nonexistent. "It is so hard to prove that cross-cultural training improves performance and productivity. If increased employee success and productivity from this training could be measured, then training departments would have criteria to sell the importance of multicultural training to top management. A control group should be set up and provided cross-cultural training and then compared to a group who is not given this training. Of course, the study would need to include pre-training testing and post-training testing and an evaluation at the end of an expatriate assignment. This type of training evaluation is always difficult, but it would be very valuable."

The faster a company can have indigenous training in the local country organization, the more effective that training becomes. Copeland believes, "You cannot run a successful training program from the United States alone. The best training is localized and run by managers from that country. As multicultural training opportunities increase, I believe there will be more emphasis on multinational effectiveness and big-picture training in specific cultures for more employees. Also, we do not do a good job of using our successful expatriates as a cadre to train others in the skills they have learned. Usually, after their transfer back to home base, they are immediately absorbed into the workforce, and the value of their experience is lost to other corporate employees. Unfortunately, this is true in many other corporations as well.

"Another point that corporations often miss is the preparation the receiving organization should make before an expatriate is transferred or a manager travels to that location. Just as the individual is prepared for the culture change, so the receiving site should be prepared with specific expectations and outcomes of the transfer," Copeland explains. "It would be interesting if companies would design a time-off-for-good-behavior model. The expatriates would have the responsibility to recruit and develop their replacements. Then when the replacements performed at the same level of competence, the expatriate would return to home base. If a successful transfer was made in record time, then the expatriate could be rewarded with an early return to the home base," Copeland suggests.

THE IMPORTANCE OF GLOBAL TRAINING

Integrating Global Issues into Other Training Courses

The ultimate objective of a multicultural training program is not to develop a curriculum in global, but to find approaches and processes to build sensitivity to global issues into any training. This more comprehensive approach can be implemented after a corporation has successfully experienced specific multicultural sessions in cultural awareness, multinational communication, and cross-cultural training. An example of this type of integration is provided in the simulation STRATCO from the BJ Chakiris Corporation and Management Simulations described in Figure 5–2.[67]

International Training for Competition

With so much at stake, from the success of business negotiations to the effective operation of global subsidiaries or joint ventures, there is little rationale for not investing time and money in training employees who must work in a global workforce. The training costs are small compared to the potential costs of early returns from expatriate assignments or business losses due to the lack of multicultural competency. As with any training, top-management support is imperative. American senior executives must start initiating and supporting companywide global training programs.

In addition to the gains in productivity and profits influenced by global training, corporations may want to consider the issue from a social perspective as well. "The military trains its soldiers before sending them into battle, churches educate and train their missionaries before sending them out to proselytize, and governments train secret agents before they go under cover; but U.S. firms send employees overseas cold," say Black and Mendenhall.[68] Such a sink-or-swim

FIGURE 5–2
STRATCO

Client originally developed for:	Problem/business issue:	Intended result:	Targeted audience:
A world-class manufacturing group of a multinational high-technology conglomerate.	Integrate expertise on three continents to produce automobile subsystems using existing manufacturing facilities.	Teach managers how to coordinate action between management teams.	Senior-operation managers from the component plants within the group's divisions.

CONTENT: Coordination, situation analysis, strategy development, implementation planning, financial analysis, budgeting, market segmentation, product life cycle, manpower planning, product development, and competitive analysis.

SCENARIO: Models a diversified component manufacturer supplying parts and subsystems to a hypothetical "point of sale" terminal industry. The company consists of a head-quarters team and three to five division teams. Division teams compete in distinct markets—printer, displays, keyboards, scanners, and communication. Each division team competes against three major competitors in its market, and each market is unique from the others in its size, growth, buying patterns, etc. The products are sold in three large international markets. The headquarters team is given the task of setting financial policy for all teams, giving cash to divisions in fast-growing markets that need money to expand production, and taking cash from profitable slow-growth divisions. The headquarters team must also invent a new miniterminal division that will offer hand-held terminals using components from all its divisions.

COMMUNICATION: The headquarters team develops a mission statement, global strategic direction, and corporate financial goals. It reviews the strategies and performance of each of the divisions by holding meetings, writing memos, or calling divisions on the telephone.

Division teams make product positioning, marketing, production, and manpower decisions. Since they are embroiled in a hotly contested marketplace of their own, their fortunes are closely linked to the financial goals and capital decisions made by headquarters. At the end of the simulation the class is brought together and asked to compare its actions in the simulation with its behavior in the real world and with its conception of how a world-class organization should interact.

DELIVERY TECHNOLOGY: Teams use microcomputers and Lotus 1-2-3 spreadsheets to implement a strategy. Spreadsheets include R&D, marketing, production, human resources, finance, and proforma financial statements. Each round represents one year of real time. Teams are connected by telephone and have baskets that raise coordination issues. All teams receive an industry newsletter that describes events in all of the marketplaces.

CUSTOMIZATION: This simulation can lend itself to many applications, including strategic planning, team building, and group integration. It can be easily customized to fit unique needs and market environment.

approach would seem irresponsible and unreasonable to the military, clergy, or government. Why then does it seem logical to the business sector?

If U.S. firms are to compete successfully in what is becoming a global battleground, they must provide their employees with the ammunition and weapons necessary to fight effective and victorious campaigns.

Chapter Six

Selecting and Training Global Managers and Trainers

Let us not be blind to our differences, but let us direct our attention to our common interest and to the means by which those differences can be resolved. And if we cannot end now our differences, at least we can make the world safe for diversity.

—John F. Kennedy

As companies increasingly compete in a world marketplace, they are transferring more employees across national boundaries. The high cost of an overseas assignment and high failure rates place a premium on selecting the right candidate. At IBM, international management development starts with smart recruiting. Donald Laidlaw, IBM's former director of executive resources and management development, says the corporation has become more selective over the years about the people it sends on international assignments. "We're trying to be more sensitive and careful. We're giving more consideration to the individual's potential. We're considering the value of the assignment, both to the individual and to the business."[1]

Because the corporation invests time and money on preparing the trainer for an international assignment, the recruiting factor is equally important in the selection of global trainers.

THE SELECTION PROCESS

IOR Survey

To better understand the selection of candidates for expatriate assignments, International Orientation Resources (IOR) conducted a survey of *Fortune* 500 multinational companies. It faxed questionnaires to human resource professionals in 78 corporations. Follow-up calls were made to record the responses. Responses were received from international human resources specialists from 50 companies, a 64 percent response rate.[2]

The companies surveyed were asked to specify what criteria they used to select their candidates for global assignments.

The most common selection criteria (listed in order of importance) were:

- Technical expertise.
- Management ability.
- Previous overseas experience.
- Personality profiles.
- Language skills.
- Previous successful work.
- Cultural sensitivity.
- Career potential.
- Company experience.
- Interpersonal skills.
- Flexibility.

Other criteria mentioned included: interpersonal skills, team orientation, health, family situation, flexibility, availability, formal education, and cost.

Technical expertise was the most important selection criterion, identified by nearly 90 percent of the responding companies. Management ability was also designated by more than 50 percent of the respondents. The ranking order for global trainers would probably be much the same although presentation skills should be added and would rank within the top five criteria.

These results are not surprising since technical expertise is essential for most international positions and is easily measured. Similarly, management ability is assessed through performance reviews. Other criteria such as cultural sensitivity and flexibility, however, are much more difficult to evaluate.

They are often analyzed in a cursory manner or forgotten entirely, especially when the selection process is performed under time constraints.

What methods are used for selection? The most common methods respondents reported for selection are:

- Performance evaluation.
- Interviews.
- References.
- Written instruments.
- Host-country request.
- Successful expatriate profiles.
- Career development assessment.
- No formal procedure.

More than 50 percent of the responding companies in the selection process used both performance evaluations and interviews. Career development assessments were used by only 8 percent of the respondents' surveyed corporations.

In response to the question, "What do you consider to be the most reliable selection procedures?" 14 percent of the respondents said that no single selection procedure is best. The results showed interviews, performance reviews, and references at the top of the list. Half of those respondents who named specific methods in their answer named only a single method—the remaining 50 percent chose multiple methods.

Two firms active in assisting corporations in the selection of managers for expatriate assignments provide more detailed insight into the selection process for trainers as well. These two companies are Moran, Stahl & Boyer International (MS&B International) and Selection Research International, Inc. (SRI).

MS&B International Services

MS&B International recognizes the challenge of identifying, recruiting, selecting, and developing expatriates for global companies.[3] To deploy the best people on international assignments, the focus of expatriate selection has to move beyond assessment of job and technical qualifications. This change is essential because expatriate assignments fail primarily due to spouse and employee cultural maladjustment and family difficulties rather than an employee's lack of technical qualifications. Companies that consider the cross-cultural adaptability of the employee and spouse in their selection and development programs are likely to avoid costly failures.

MS&B International offers two cross-cultural assessment tools. The International Assignment Assessment Service uses a self-response questionnaire, the Overseas Assignment Inventory (OAI), for a number of assessment and developmental applications. This inventory measures a variety of attitudes and attributes that are important to cross-cultural adjustment. It is a standardized instrument that provides direct and comparable information across candidates. When the inventory is used, the entire range of expatriate assessment and development activities is anchored in objective and relevant information, and not in gut feelings or best guesses. The OAI can be an important part of your international human resource planning and management process by helping you assess the cross-cultural adaptability of potential global trainers.

The OAI is a paper-and-pencil instrument that measures 15 areas of motivations, expectations, attitudes, and attributes that have been proven necessary for successful cross-cultural adaptation and performance. It is flexible in its applications. The most common applications currently are for expatriate selection and development.

Selection

When a company is considering a candidate for an international assignment, the OAI is administered to the candidate and his or her spouse. The instruments are scored and a private time is scheduled with each couple for a structured behavioral assessment interview based on the OAI. The interviewer(s) need to be certified OAI users, be skilled in the art of behavioral interviewing, and have an in-depth knowledge of the destination culture. Emphasis on verification of the inventory scores through interview findings is important in this process. After the conclusion of the interview, the interviewer assesses and evaluates the information from the interview and makes an objective judgment regarding the cross-cultural suitability of the couple. The findings are then presented to the company.

Development

The OAI can also be used effectively as a tool to develop and prepare employees to become effective global managers or trainers. One application is to administer the instrument to employees who have an international assignment as an identified step in their career development plan. It is certainly preferable if spouses participate in this development process from the beginning stage. Each person's OAI profile is reviewed by a qualified interviewer. Through a structured developmental interview, individuals gain a better understanding of their own strengths and areas in need of further development. Based on the OAI and other available information, if candidacy continues to be a possibility after assessment, specific developmental goals and objectives are identified by the company in collaboration with the employee. Throughout the process, the employee's progress against the development plan is jointly monitored by the employee and the company. Within a year or more, if the employee has made significant progress against the development plan (to his or her own, and the company's satisfaction) and if an assignment is pending, he or she completes inventory again. This time, the OAI is coupled with a behavioral interview that is site specific. However, if there has been no significant progress against the development plan, the likelihood of candidacy for an international assignment is diminished.

SRI Services

SRI of St. Louis, Missouri, is another firm that offers selection consulting.[4] Its organizational services focus on two important related areas: international personnel assessment and organizational planning and management development. These services include auditing the corporate international human resources function, analyzing organization and management needs, and developing tailored action plans for organization development, research, and planning.

For organizations, SRI offers:

- Global Manpower Integration—integrating domestic high-potential management programs with international staffing needs and creating leadership data pools of foreign national managers in world areas.

- Assessing individual employees in relation to specific organizational needs and international projects, including human resources planning, career development, and succession planning.

On an individual basis, SRI:

- Helps the employees and spouses make informed decisions about accepting a foreign assignment by helping them to focus on personal, family, and career issues and by providing counseling when needed.

- Identifies pre-assignment training and development needs—providing information for managing the employee's in-country assignment and giving special support to the spouse and/or accompanying dependents.

Assessment Services

Assessment procedures focus on employee suitability for a specific international training assignment, including how well the employee fits the position for contributing to the organization's objectives and the potential for the employee, spouse, and dependent children to adjust successfully to the foreign environment.

Clients receive a behavioral assessment of the employee and spouse following the assessment through discussions with senior management and a written evaluation report. SRI's assessment procedures also provide information to senior management about employees identified as high-potential managers or future training candidates. This information is in such areas as leadership skills, temperament, communication styles, and social intelligence, as well as the ability to function effectively as a manager in a cross-cultural environment. This information is especially valuable for the trainer.

In circumstances where a corporation is already sophisticated in its evaluation approach and its human resource staff possesses requisite background and skills, SRI provides training in specific aspects of its research-based assessment procedures.

When SRI's assessment procedures are used as a management thinking model, they have many uses:

- Evaluating selected employees and spouses for country-specific assignments.
- Determining developmental assignments for managers.
- Establishing a bridge between the high-potential manager group (future leaders) and the global management group.
- Evaluating trainers for their capacity to adjust and work effectively in a foreign culture and their strengths and deficits (triggering areas for preparation and trainer training).

Cross-cultural researchers have identified the following characteristics as key predictors for successful international adjustment: empathy, respect, interest in local cultures, flexibility, tolerance, initiative, and self-esteem.

There are two fundamentals that SRI's research emphasizes. One is the candidate's commitment to the job—the individual gets a sense of self-satisfaction from doing the work. Second, when confronted by the complexities of the interpersonal dimension, the individual does not become self-serving. Although intelligence is important, it is less important than social intelligence (the domain of empathy, insight, and introspection that gets translated into action). This is the area where alliances are built and people cooperate to achieve goals.

Assessing the International Training Candidate and Spouse

Pre-Evaluation.

1. Needs Analysis—SRI staff meets with the client to obtain an overview of the foreign assignment, job context, and job description and to discuss the client's requirements and what needs to be included in the written evaluation report.

2. Reference Interview—When it is possible, SRI personnel would like to speak, by telephone, with a past supervisor, peer, or subordinate who has worked with the candidate within the organization and who has been designated and contacted by the candidate for this purpose.

3. Overview and Questionnaire—SRI provides the client with a written overview of the evaluation process for distribution to the candidate and spouse. SRI personnel also like to speak with the participants prior to their assessment about their questions and concerns and send them background information form(s), which participants fill out and bring to the session.

4. Briefing—SRI begins the assessment process with a brief orientation to the day's activities. During the briefing the participants are encouraged to discuss their expectations and concerns about the assessment process and the international assignment. The candidate and spouse are asked to sign a release form authorizing SRI to share the results of the assessment with the client.

Evaluation Procedures.

5. Background Information Form—This questionnaire provides information relevant to cultural adjustment and job fit.

6. Testing—The Jackson Personality Inventory (JPI) is a professionally developed, standardized psychometric test. Its behavioral dimensions have been correlated with SRI's research. The test is administered separately to the candidate and spouse. It is scored and analyzed during the session, and the results are used in the interview process.

7. Interviews—The candidate and spouse receive separate focused adaptability interviews; areas that are flagged by the JPI, background information forms, and reference interview(s) are probed for significant, relevant information.

8. Cross-Cultural Videotapes—During the interview process, the person not being interviewed is shown two videotapes. The first covers overseas adjustment issues and their effect on the individual and family unit; the second deals with the reentry issues one faces on returning home.

9. Joint Couple Interview and Wrap-Up—At the conclusion of the assessment, SRI personnel meet with the candidate and spouse to discuss their questions and concerns, address issues raised during the session, and continue probing. SRI also provides counseling to help them make an informed self-selection decision as well as recommendations for preparing themselves, if they are selected.

10. Focused Adaptability and Behavioral Assessment Report—Following the assessment procedures, SRI discusses the results with the client and generates a written evaluation report. This assessment evaluates the candidate's and spouse's ability to adapt to a country-specific environment. The report may include a go/no go decision and recommendations for affecting a successful transfer, support, and management of the employee and his/her spouse and children while located abroad.

   The report contains a comprehensive assessment of the candidate's and spouse's personality attributes and patterns of family interaction and the potential impact of these attributes and patterns on job fit, performance, and overseas adaptability. It may also contain information about the need for additional screening. When used for career and organizational planning, SRI's assessment procedures can be used to identify areas for additional management training and development.

11. Confidentiality—Information obtained by SRI is kept in strictest confidence. It is shared only with personnel authorized by the client to receive verbal feedback and written information about the assessment. At the beginning of the assessment session SRI requests the person(s) being evaluated to sign a release form(s). The release form permits SRI to give to the client pertinent information obtained by the assessment procedures.

Figure 6–1 shows a sample SRI Candidate Profile form, and Figure 6–2 demonstrates how behavioral anchors are ranked. Figure 6–3 presents SRI's Competency Driven Master Plan.

A few corporations are looking at providing internal assessment services for the selection of global managers and trainers. At the present time, however, most of the assessments used by global corporations are conducted by external consulting firms. In addition. here are two other innovative programs that might prove helpful in the global selection area: the Expatriate Profile and the Interchange Program.

Expatriate Profile

An interesting personalized approach to expatriate assessment is the Expatriate Profile designed by Roger L. M. Dunbar and Allan Bird, professors at New York University.[5] This is an interactive, self-managed, computer-based

FIGURE 6–1
SRI's Candidate Profile

International Candidate and Spouse Profile

Traits
- Maturity/emotional stability
- Introspection
- Intelligence
- Social intelligence
- Flexibility/adaptability
- Tolerance
- Interpersonal skills
- Motivation
- Values/ethics
- Responsibility
- Independence/confidence
- Marital satisfaction

---

training program that provides information for the individual who has never been abroad or participated in an expatriate assignment. It provides a simulation of the types of issues and questions that a person assigned overseas may expect to have to deal with.

To use the computer program, the user enters his or her name into the computer and is asked a variety of questions. To work through the first exercises, the individual needs to select a specific country and know statistics about the company, such as the company's market share and percentage of revenue in the chosen country. As the user provides information in response to the program's queries, the session focuses on the user and the concerns likely to arise as a result of his or her particular assignment. The program is flexible in that it can cope with a combination of factors and issues involving approximately 150 different countries.

Such an exploration will enable managers to make anticipatory adjustments that are likely to increase their level of comfort in carrying out their new assignments. The primary objective of the profile is to point out different

FIGURE 6–2
SRI's Employee Summary Profile

Traits	Behavioral Anchors				
	1	2	3	4	5
• Maturity/emotional stability					
• Introspection					
• Intelligence					
• Social intelligence					
• Flexibility/adaptability					
• Tolerance					
• Interpersonal skills					
• Motivation					
• Values/ethics					
• Responsibility					
• Independence/confidence					
• Marital satisfaction					

Ranking:

1 Well-suited for assignment.

2 Suited for assignment.
Minimal preparation/development

3 Meets minimum. Development indicated.

4 Below minimum. Requires substantial
development. Potential knock-out factor.

5 Knock-out factor. Below minimum.
Development not appropriate.

sources of change and to raise questions as to whether it is possible to take steps that will help expatriates cope with these expected changes.

A second objective of the Expatriate Profile is to help trainers consider which among various adjustment modes are the most appropriate in their new situation. Confronted with alternative ways of doing things, it sometimes makes sense to adjust to the local way. This is not always the case, however, because situations exist where it is more effective to avoid an issue completely and/or withdraw. Again, the aim of the program is to make participants aware of the different choices that are available.

The Expatriate Profile is used to test some ideas about what possibly may work and to explore how both the participant and the situation might be influenced by certain initiatives or changes.

FIGURE 6–3
SRI Competency Driven Master Plan

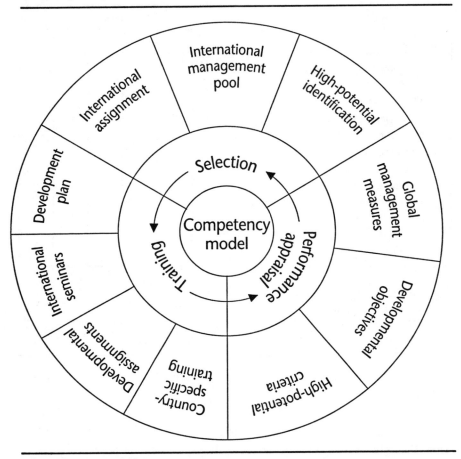

Source: Selection Research International, Inc., 1992.

The Interchange Program

A program developed by Interchange International for company managers could be effectively used for trainers or training managers before they begin an international assignment.[6] Interchange is an international company that specializes in arranging two-month developmental assignments in noncompeting corporations for key managers. Client firms participate actively in selecting an American, multinational, or foreign company and in designing and tailoring work assignments for their manager. The objective is to return a manager to the organization 60 days later, with both an unparalleled developmental experience and a grasp of host-company expertise. For potential global trainers, this could provide a short-term assignment to assess effectiveness for international company positions.

The Interchange program was designed in 1981 within the Volvo Car Corporation in Gothenburg, Sweden. Since then, Volvo has placed more than 200 managers in Interchange assignments in more than 100 companies around the world.[7]

The driving force behind Interchange has been an American, Bob Kelly, who, in 1981, headed Volvo's management development department. Kelly left Volvo in 1987 and formed Interchange International to offer this service to other corporations.

In 1988, Interchange U.K. was opened in London and then Interchange U.S.A. was launched. The Interchange network and its experiences and contacts with several hundred host companies, make possible the special access and responsible management essential to Interchange's effectiveness and reliability.

Purpose

The purpose of an Interchange assignment is to drop the participant for 60 days into an unfamiliar organizational culture, in which he or she must learn to perform effectively enough to return with an agreed-upon outcome needed by the participant's own organization.

The task is to isolate, understand, and bring home a competitive-edge capability from the host company. This capability should be valued and sought by the participant's organization. The participant is responsible for navigating the new culture and taking the initiatives required to complete this assignment within the two-month time frame.

The assignment is designed as a breakthrough experience, surpassing the power of traditional techniques of management development and competitive benchmarking to produce both stronger managers and more significant innovation. The Interchange assignment is known for developing:

- Individual resourcefulness.
- Accelerated learning skills.
- Self-confidence.
- Revitalized commitment.
- Successful transfer of innovative ideas.

Objectives

To achieve the assignment's purpose, the participant must meet four objectives:

- Get in (Position yourself to achieve the objective of the assignment.)
- Pick up (Define, acquire, and transfer out the desired outcome.)
- Give back (Contribute equivalent value to the host organization.)
- Sell across (Persuade your organization to act on the new ideas.)

Program Management

Interchange U.S.A. manages the contact and arrangements for each Interchange experience, based on objectives and host-company selections made by the candidate and the client organization. It does this in cooperation with the Interchange International network.

Interchange interviews and counsels the candidates, their managers, and the management development staff professionals on the selection of a host company and the assignment. Interchange develops an agreement on the individual's and company's objectives for the international assignment. Then, it arranges the placement and introduces the candidate to contact personnel in the host company to jointly design the two-month assignment. Also, Interchange conducts a launch seminar for a group of candidates before the assignment and a debriefing and reentry seminar at the conclusion.

The candidate is responsible for selecting targeted host organizations that would provide both access to some business expertise of value and a learning experience tailored to the candidate's developmental needs. The candidate must attend the launch seminar before carrying out the two-month assignment. Following the assignment the candidate attends the debrief/reentry seminar and prepares an action plan to implement new ideas gained from the Interchange experience.

The client company's human resource organization is responsible for facilitating the selection of candidates, obtaining the internal commitment needed, and arranging the planning interview with Interchange U.S.A.

Results

The Interchange experience provides four kinds of results that are often promised and seldom delivered by other approaches.

First, a quantum jump results from a culture shock experience. The manager or trainer is more open to change and aware of alternative approaches in a new culture.

Second, innovative techniques for closing a gap or creating an edge in the client company's capability—techniques that have been proven in another organization and evaluated and adapted by the Interchange manager—are effectively introduced into the client organization.

Third, a highly motivating rotational strategy for both fast-trackers who need broadening and vision and for plateaued but valuable managers who need a high-impact, regenerating assignment.

Finally, trainers or managers who take Interchange assignments with an international organization would experience a hands-on sense of the cultural and operating issues of international management and competition— without the cost, career risk, and talent diversion of a traditional overseas assignment.

Dual-Career Couples

Noel Kreicker, president of IOR, has studied the impact of the dual-career couple on the international assignment.[8] As growing numbers of high-potential candidates with career-oriented spouses are slated for international assignments, the challenge of expatriating the dual-career couple becomes significantly greater. There are no simple guidelines for responding appropriately to the financial and professional pressures faced by the expatriating dual-career couple. This is also a concern with the selection of trainers and training managers.

In the U.S. culture, employees' primary identities are related to their career. In other cultures, identity may be based on the status of education and social position. The opportunities for the spouse to continue employment in the assigned country are slim. Therefore, when partners give up careers to accompany their spouses to another country, they are giving up their primary identity. The result is a significant role change for the accompanying spouse. Tough though it is, some couples prefer to opt for a commuter marriage rather than career interruption.

Another major factor is the income loss. Unfortunately, companies may not compensate the couple for loss of the spouse's income during the expatriate assignment. With the lower income, the expatriates' lifestyle may be more modest in the assigned country than in the United States. The feelings of shared partnership and equal status may be lessened when one partner stops working. Also, becoming dependent upon the employed spouse for financial support is often a source of conflict. Thus, the marriage dynamic may shift significantly in the relocation.

Corporations know that this problem is complex and are eager for solutions to the dilemma. Some firms provide spouses with job searches in regions where spouse employment is legal. Sometimes the corporation provides positions for the spouses and hires them during the assignment period. Other firms pay legal fees for spouses to obtain work permits in the new country. A few companies provide spouses with a yearly allowance to be spent on travel, professional conferences, or continuing education fees.

IOR provides preparation and training for the expatriate dual-career couple. The dual-career focus of IOR's cross-cultural training program begins with a needs analysis of the expatriating couple. A first area of focus is to determine the career history of the trailing spouse and his or her expectations for future employment and/or other possible options. To gain perspective about the spouse's career, the interviewer asks questions such as:

- What was the career plan before the international assignment became a reality?
- Where is the couple now in relation to the plan?
- Are there alternate tracks on the career path?
- What options to enhance their careers are they aware of in the destination city?

IOR's dual-career training program begins with clarifying objectives for the program. Some couples may already have decided on a strategy for the international assignment. For example, they might have agreed that it is an ideal time to begin a family. Others look forward to a pause in their career, a time to step back and develop outside interests. Most couples come into the training with considerable frustration. Because the issues surrounding the sacrifice of one's career for another's are highly volatile, partners are relieved to begin building an effective framework for discussion in the safe environment of the training room.

Typical course objectives are:

- Understanding the impact of the move on each partner.
- Setting strategies for mutual support in the new environment.
- Clarifying the reality of the spouse's options in the host country.
- Learning about tangibles overseas: specific facts and names related to the spouse's area of interest.
- Determining ways to stay professionally current while overseas.
- Planning for reentering the workforce upon repatriation.

Once the objectives are clarified and prioritized, the couple is encouraged to:

- Identify strengths, individually and as a couple.
- Assess goals, individually and as a couple.
- Understand major concerns of dual-career families.
- Examine options and acquire specific information for the spouse.
- Understand the new culture as it relates to each person's professional aspirations.
- Develop strategies, individually and as a couple.
- Commit to an action plan.

Corporations providing such programs realize the cost benefits of supporting dual-career couples and helping them in the success of the expatriate assignment.

THE TRAINING PROCESS

Now that we have addressed the selection of trainers and managers for international assignments, let's discuss how to prepare them for global training positions.

Cultural Differences

At the top of any list of skills necessary for a successful global trainer is the understanding of cultural differences. William D. Shea, director of the Center for Creative Leadership's European office in Brussels, Belgium, presents an interesting perspective on culture, especially as it pertains to the European area.[9]

Defining culture is not any easier for Europeans than for North Americans. Over the past year, Shea has had the opportunity to talk with many training professionals on the topic of cultural diversity. He has identified a working definition of culture: the rules we live by. This notion includes the way we see the world and the way we make sense of what we see.

Shea presents some interesting comments representative of some of the thoughts and feelings shared during his discussions with training professionals. The ideas are to be viewed as a starting point or a springboard against which to test new observations and ideas.

- Cultural diversity should not be confused with nationality. There is a tendency in Europe to talk about differences between north and south or differences between France and Germany. The reality seems to be that there are a number of cultures within each country.
- People learn to operate in ways that are different from their original culture but, under stress, revert to their original ways. This is as true for an individual in a marriage as it is for managers in a foreign country.
- Understanding cultures is among the most critical factors in the ultimate success of a merger. This is true of companies from within a country but is even more critical when the companies are from different countries.
- When entering a new culture, it is unwise to imitate the people. Individuals must begin by being themselves while watching for differences to emerge.
- There is a philosophical understanding among those who manage diversity that the process begins with self-understanding. To state this more succinctly, the deeper one goes inside oneself, the greater the capacity to understand someone else.
- To successfully enter into another culture, one person should focus on the ability of the group to accomplish its tasks and the other observer should provide information on group process. Apparently, this method is used by Japanese managers entering new cultures.
- Some people within global organizations believe that a company's culture may be as determined by the rules, procedures, and processes of the parent company as by the culture of the country in which the company is located. This is an interesting proposition that is worthy of further investigation. If it is true, one would serve one's clients as much by helping them understand the culture of the parent company as by understanding the country's culture. This is not an either/or issue but one requiring attention to both.
- When Person A behaves in ways that violate Person B's culture, a variety of reactions may occur. The important thing is to look for cues that indicate the response. Some people confront others while others withdraw. It raises questions about the mechanisms and practices that allow us to learn from others regarding our own behavior and its effect on others.

Shea also projects implications for training and development programs.
- Programs about cultural diversity should begin by establishing the common ground among participants. Programs that begin with differences are typically met with a backlash; participants protest the differences

because they recognize common interests and values. At this point, important differences can get swept under the rug.

- Pedagogical differences are important to acknowledge if a person wants to succeed in Europe. Europeans prefer dialogue to monologue. They are particularly sensitive to North Americans *preaching* management practices. They want opportunities to discuss and react. This is particularly true for instrument-driven programs. Programs with instruments are relatively new, therefore caution is required.

- Europeans are similar to North Americans in that they want to participate as well as listen. Feedback on a person's own behavior seems to be a new concept, particularly feedback from a person's subordinates. For some people, asking subordinates for feedback is considered an unusual practice.

- Programs that only sell insights ultimately will not sell. More insight does not automatically translate into new behaviors.

- Many Europeans resent their sites being treated as branch plants. Those who market North American programs should be sensitive to this point.

- When listening to European managers discuss the issues they are facing, Shea is struck with the similarity to the concerns of North American managers. However, he has learned not to presuppose this similarity but listen to the ideas as they are presented.

- European organizations express concern about the impact of the European Community. They are concerned about competition and losing protection. Leadership development during this time must focus on reassuring people about their ability to proceed into the future. Having a vision about how to proceed is also an issue.

- There is a perception by management consultants that Eastern Europe is being managed by economists and accountants. As the desire is to move toward a market-based economy, management people worry that the bureaucrats will not succeed. They argue that effort must be expended to help managers learn leadership skills because change can not be artificially orchestrated by economists.

Finally, Shea believes that people who will be most successful at managing cultural diversity are those people who are most comfortable with themselves. Think about people who are comfortable working between boundaries. Think about people who are able to cross functional lines. Think about people who are curious and excited about difference of any kind. The common denominator is confidence that comes from self-understanding and acceptance.

Skills Global Trainers Need

To determine what characteristics are necessary for successful overseas management, IOR distributed surveys to 400 long-term expatriate managers of different nationalities in January 1990.[10]

Seventy-four percent of the global managers were Americans or Canadians whose time spent abroad averaged 10 years. Twenty percent were Europeans who had been expatriates for an average of 11 years, and 6 percent were other nationalities—generally Asians and Latin Americans—who had lived overseas for an average of 8 years.

In the survey, the global managers were asked:

- What skills they need to be effective overseas.
- What challenges they face.
- What they predict for the future.
- How they would advise their successors.
- What challenges expatriates will probably have to face in the 1990s.

Four skills were considered essential by global managers of many different nationalities: patience, flexibility in action and thought, the ability to listen well, and the ability to learn foreign languages. These skills are also crucial ones for trainers and human resource managers.

- Flexibility—How well will the person adapt to different cultures and working situations?
- Patience—In international assignments, progress is often made much more slowly than at the home office. Is the expatriate comfortable working at a slower pace?
- Good listening skills—Often, good ideas can be stated in unfamiliar ways. Is the expatriate willing to listen to what is being said?
- Language ability—Native fluency is not necessary. However, the expatriate will be accepted more readily by local nationals if he or she has some capacity in the local language.

Other skills often considered essential include: teambuilding with people of other nationalities, committing to the long term, and exhibiting a respect for the local people and their customs—both socially and in business. Presentation and facilitation skills are equally essential skills for training professionals.

A major training area for the global trainer is intercultural communication. In *Basics of Intercultural Communication* these factors include: language, place, thought processing, and nonverbal communication.[11]

Language

- Accent—An accent is the way an individual pronounces, enunciates, and articulates words. Trainers and managers should understand what an accent does or does not indicate about an individual's education, degree of assimilation into the host culture, and ability to understand the language.
- Linguistics—Some linguistics experts believe that language shapes the way the culture uses it—basically influencing the way its speakers think.
- Translation—Translation presents difficulties such as gross translation errors and nuance errors.

Place—in the intercultural sense: the existing technological level of the culture and the physical environment

- Personal space—The way individuals use space varies greatly from culture to culture.
- Technology—Americans and Western Europeans must remember that a low level of technological sophistication may be the deliberate choice of a particular country.

Thought Processing

- Social Organization—Intercultural conflicts often arise when an individual's views of the social organization in which he or she operates are seen as universal.
- Contexting—Contexting is the way in which one communicates and the circumstances surrounding the communication.
- Authority—Whether an individual has the ability or inclination to act on his or her own initiative also is culturally determined.
- Concept of time—A cultural concept of time includes the importance a culture places on time and its philosophy toward the past, present, and future.

Nonverbal Behavior

- Appearance
- Body language
- Touching
- Eye contact

Challenges

When IOR asked global managers what their greatest professional challenges are, most Americans responded: accepting less efficiency, expecting change too quickly, and accepting a different work ethic. Essentially these three difficulties can be condensed into one major challenge—accepting the fact that not everyone in the world works the way you do.[12]

Often, new expatriate training directors do not understand that the host culture largely determines which management style will work. Training managers who have been highly successful at home become frustrated when their productivity level decreases. They must accept that, in another country, they are personally less efficient than in their own culture. "You cannot impose your [work] methods throughout the world and expect to get the same results [as at home]," one respondent advised.

Basically, the consensus was that expatriates' productivity cannot peak until they understand the host-country's cultural values and management structure. Expatriates must be careful not to blame the host-country's customs for any difficulties they encounter. "What is wrong with these people and their culture?" "Why can't they understand me?" These are questions many expatriate trainers ask. This approach will not break down the cultural barriers that block progress. With such a narrow perspective, trainers cannot hope to gain an understanding of the local culture. Overcoming this perspective is a major challenge.

Realistic Goals

Arash Afshar of International Consultants for Management and Development points out that an international assignment involves transition expectations.[13] The expatriate's emotional stages move on a continuum: excitement, apprehension, realization, acceptance, and settlement.

Employees going on international assignments should have realistic expectations about what they can accomplish both personally and professionally.

Realistic goals include:

- Setting realistic goals so that they don't become frustrated or disillusioned. The challenges peculiar to the international assignment may require reevaluation of the goals during that time.
- Maintaining positive, steady emotions. An expatriate assignment can have many emotional highs and lows. The expatriate who understands this in advance is better prepared to deal with these emotions in a balanced way.

- Updating skills continuously. What can expatriates bring back from the assignment that will help them to grow in their careers?

Jean Michel Boisvert, training analyst for the Department of National Revenue in Québec, Canada, advises trainers to put into practice the words of Ghandi: "Go to the people, start with what they are, build on what they have."[14] By doing this, the trainer will walk with participants, guide them, and assist them in their new discovery. Then all interventions will come from an attitude of mutual respect.

Boisvert identifies these techniques as necessary for a successful global manager or trainer:

- Counseling skills—such as active listening and empathy.
- Nonverbal behavior—what nonverbal language is appropriate in each culture.
- Communication styles—passive, assertive, and aggressive behavior and which is appropriate or inappropriate for a particular culture.
- Communication strategy—how a course will be presented to participants.
- Knowledge of the topic to be taught—awareness of latest theories and practices on the course topic area.
- Adaptability to tailor course material for the participants' cultural environment.
- Strong questioning ability—to help participants discover meaning for themselves.

Beverly Geber, associate editor of *Training* magazine, advises global trainers to:[15]

- Understand that work may proceed at a slower pace and a lower quality standard than they desire.
- Employ, wherever possible, a multicultural staff in order to benefit from the advantages of a diverse perspective.
- Focus on human relations as the key to developing trust and loyalty with foreign national contacts and colleagues.
- Know their own culture as the basis for respecting and understanding another culture.

While technical knowledge is important to success anywhere in the world, cultural understanding and cross-cultural communication skills are equally critical for success in a multicultural environment. The globalization of businesses is increasing the numbers of employees working internationally. These employees are managing multicultural staffs and cannot operate effectively unless they understand the local culture. With increased global competition, corporations are demanding more of their employees. Those trainers, human resource managers, and managers in general with international experience who can function effectively in multicultural environments will be in demand and will lead the way for successful multinational corporations.

Effective Training for Global Trainers

Some companies believe that the only way to develop global trainers and managers is to let them work in many cultures and countries. Others say that anyone can acquire the global skills necessary through effective international training programs. Still others support the view that choosing an employee from the specific country and culture and providing them with the training skills is the best approach for global training. John Fulkerson, vice president of organization and management development for Pepsi-Cola International in Somers, New York, belongs to the group that says you can't grow real global managers in a cultural vacuum.[16] "It's difficult to have that understanding without living in another culture. You can have some understanding by reading, but you can't have that gut-level understanding without working across borders," he says.

Trainers conducting training programs in other countries experience challenges they never encounter at home. Once expatriates accept international assignments, they are going to be changed for the rest of their lives because they're going to look at things differently. Fulkerson continues, "For example, you might not get upset about not being able to get a call through for 10 minutes, because it used to take two hours in another country."

According to a study by The Conference Board, corporations have made some significant changes in their approach to international job assignments in order to develop a global perspective in employees.[17] Among the 130 companies surveyed, 112 were U.S.-based multinationals, 12 were based in Europe, and six in Asia.

Starting Early

Johnson & Johnson has a unique program for selecting and training global managers that could be equally as effective for trainers and human resource managers. The company recruits MBA graduates from U.S.

schools who are natives of the countries where company subsidiaries are located. "We realize that the transition from student life to work culture is usually accompanied by anxiety, overconfidence, or a mixture of both," states Irene DeNigris, international recruitment and development program administrator.[18] "Add to that the cultural issues the new employee faces, and it can be confusing at best. So we contracted with International Training Associates of Princeton (ITAP International) to develop a training program presenting an introduction to the world of management to these new employees from many different countries and cultures," DeNigris explains. Conducted within Johnson & Johnson's orientation program, course objectives are to:

- Help participants make the transition from the concept-driven world of academia to the professional world of business.
- Examine the demands and responsibilities of management-related activities: planning, organization, leadership, staffing, and controlling.
- Provide a self-improvement managerial tool of management effectiveness through the lifestyle inventory.
- Review prospective work objectives and put them in perspective with the United States and home cultural and market environments.

The following are training topics and activities for this one-on-one training:

- The impact of the participant's work is discussed, including its effect on social life, schedules, status, and financial independence.
- Although most new graduates with MBAs have learned many concepts and theories about management, many students have yet to translate them into practical activities in specific terms. Each participant is challenged to establish a list of the most important tasks of a manager and then compare practices of management in the United States with practices in the home country.
- A review of communication, planning, education, and measurement practices in both worlds and bridging of the differences are presented through role playing, memo writing, critical incidents, and simulations.
- A comparative management questionnaire, "Culture in the Workplace," developed by Geert Hofstede and provided exclusively through ITAP International, gives participants a snapshot of their own management preferences and compares these with preferences of managers in those countries in which they will be working.[19] Bridging exercises are then provided to help participants work more effectively in the country of relocation.

- The participants develop an action plan with input from the overseas affiliate where they will be working. This work plan helps employees formulate ideas and address issues before they meet with supervisors to discuss setting objectives in the work environment.

The concept of recruiting students who will go back to their native countries after an American company orientation period is an innovative idea for trainers as well. The trainers would know firsthand the language and culture of their countries in addition to exposure to the U.S. culture during their school years. Add to that the knowledge of the company and the contact with corporate personnel during the orientation period and you have an employee who is culturally well-prepared for global training. Courses in presentation and communication skills, training design, and learning-style methodology could be added to the training. Students with human resource graduate degrees would be especially prepared for global training positions.

U.S. firms are also giving employees international experience much earlier than they used to. In the past, an international assignment may have hinted that the expatriate manager was being eliminated from the company career fast track. Today in many global companies, an international assignment is more likely to be an indication that the individual has high potential and is being groomed for upper-level positions.

Few companies nurture global managers better than Colgate-Palmolive.[20] Colgate earns about two-thirds of its $6 billion annual revenue from operations outside the United States. Because overseas markets have been the company's sustenance for years, international assignments are prized, and most senior managers have had some expatriate experience.

Even so, in 1987 the company decided to fine-tune its approach to recruiting and developing future managers. As a result, today it offers newly recruited graduates the choice of two company tracks.

1. Those who are eager for international assignments can get one within 18 months, after they have been properly oriented into Colgate's culture and operations.

2. The U.S. track allows new employees to begin their careers in the stateside business and move to an international assignment five or six years later.

These high potential positions are so attractive that Colgate gets about 15,000 applicants annually for only 30 positions.

Multicultural Attributes

When The Conference Board surveyed companies on successful multicultural attributes, it found a certain uniformity among U.S. and non-U.S. companies. The two success factors that tied for top place were knowledge of the business and a high degree of tolerance and flexibility. A third factor on the list was the ability to work with people. Tolerance and flexibility are especially important to global firms. Colgate emphasizes college recruiting to select candidates who already have those qualities at a young age. The company looks for four things in potential employees: work or education overseas, proficiency in a language other than English, computer skills, and some marketing, sales, or entrepreneurial experience. Although English is still considered the universal language, many companies are emphasizing the importance of trainers who speak other languages. At this point, however, most firms do not require employees to learn a foreign language.

Many U.S.-based companies discover the importance of training when they expand globally. In June 1992 with its acquisition of Carryfast, the largest private express-package service in Britain, United Parcel Service (UPS) completed its invasion of Europe.[21] This purchase, its 16th in Europe since 1987, makes the United Kingdom the 13th European country with a UPS-owned operation. It also fulfills the company's mission of establishing ground delivery operations in every major European market.

Over the years, some hard-learned lessons have prompted UPS to drastically change the way it goes about the process of melding its new ventures into the corporation. Even before the 1980s, UPS encountered problems with start-ups—especially with a green-field operation it set up in Germany in 1976. The company's experience in Germany alerted management to the challenge of blending different cultures. UPS executives discovered higher rates of absenteeism and turnover in Germany than in their American organization. When they improved the German compensation package, they began attracting a more productive workforce. UPS suffered losses for five years before sending in a team of managers to turn around the situation. Germany is one of its most profitable international operations today.

Whenever an acquisition is made, UPS brings together managers from both companies. Combining the best aspects of both companies necessitates excellent communication. According to Peter Quantrill, district manager for the United Kingdom, "I don't think you can overcommunicate when it comes to integration. You have to constantly strive to keep everybody informed about the whole process, to keep them interested, and to handle any concerns they may have during the process."[22] The company encourages communication flow through its international management training course, a two-week program held at various locations throughout Europe. The program trains participants in the UPS way of doing business and also brings together people of different cultures to share ideas in an open forum.

Timing Global Training

A study by J. Stewart Black, Hal B. Gregersen, and Mark Mendenhall points out that, although learning about cultural concepts is useful before departure, theoretical arguments support the idea that rigorous, in-depth, cross-cultural training is most effectively delivered to global managers after they have relocated.[23] Before they leave home, it is more difficult for them to understand what the trainers are trying to convey. The authors provide an example of what it is like to have a subordinate in Hong Kong say, "Yes, I understand what you want me to do" and then do nothing because in fact he or she did not understand. It is another thing to have that experience first and then learn about the cultural reasons behind that behavior in a seminar. Training in the new country has several advantages: higher participant levels of motivation, higher participant experience level with the local culture as a foundation for learning deeper cultural values and ideas, an environment where trainees can immediately apply what they learn, and the environment itself, which makes the training content real. Black, Gregersen, and Mendenhall believe that predeparture training should focus mostly on basic, day-to-day, survival-level concerns, and that firms should invest in in-country training for global managers while they are overseas. This idea is illustrated in Figure 6–4. The matrix assumes an identifiable situation for all dimensions (cultural toughness, communication toughness, and job toughness) to illustrate how stages of globalization should influence cross-cultural training design issues. In general, the more a firm is moving away from the export stage, the more rigorous the training should be. Breadth of content also increases as the firm moves away from the export stage to the global stage, and more rigorous training is needed. As firms move away from the export and multidomestic stages, global managers also need to be able to socialize host-country trainers and managers into the firm's corporate culture and other firm-specific practices. This added managerial responsibility intensifies the need for rigorous training.

Whether a firm has a pattern of globalization that requires many or few global managers to be in positions around the world, those managers need to be trained according to the contexts of their assignments. To maintain external

FIGURE 6–4
Stage of Globalization and Training Design Issues

EXPORT STAGE

Degree of rigor required is low to moderate.

Content emphasis is on interpersonal skills, local culture, consumer values, and behavior.

Low to moderate training of host nationals; focus on understanding home-country products and policies.

MULTINATIONAL STAGE

Degree of rigor required is moderate to high.

Content emphasis is on interpersonal skills, two-way technology transfer, corporate value transfer, international strategy, stress management, local culture, and business practices.

Moderate to high training of host nationals in technical areas, product/service systems, and corporate culture.

MULTIDOMESTIC STAGE

Degree of rigor required is moderate to high.

Content emphasis is on interpersonal skills, local culture, technology transfer, stress management, local business practices, and laws.

Low to moderate training of host nationals; primary focus is on production/service procedures.

GLOBAL STAGE

Degree of rigor required is moderate to high.

Content emphasis is on global corporate operations/systems, corporate culture transfer, multiple cultural values and business systems, international strategy, and socialization tactics.

High training of host nationals in global corporate production/efficiency systems, corporate culture, multiple cultural and business systems, and headquarters.

Source: J. Stewart Black, Hal B. Gregerson, and Mark Mendenhall, *Global Assignments*, San Francisco, CA, Jossey-Bass, 1992.

fit, the training function must be flexible enough to deal with all potential contexts that derive from globalization patterns. A rigid, mechanistic training philosophy will not work in the global arena. The framework offered in this chapter is a training strategy by which wise choices can be made despite constraints in the organization and the environment.

Tips for Global Trainers

Joyce Rogers, international training specialist with MCI, offers the following tips for training global trainers:[24]

1. You need to be concerned with.
   - Perceptions—How people see the world.
   - Assumptions—Underlying beliefs/values.
   - Expectations—That things will be a certain way.

2. Solicit help from people who have effectively trained in other cultures.
   - Have them create appropriate case studies.
   - Have them write critical incidents.
   - Have them help train the trainers.

3. Some required qualities for the trainers of trainers.
   - Do not have an axe to grind.
   - Do not pontificate.
   - Do not share war stories.
   - Demonstrate acculturation.
   - Be reflective.
   - Be observant.
   - Be introspective.
   - Be able to adjust to their own adjustment.

4. Select a peer as a mentor.

5. Be quiet and observe, then tailor the training.

6. Maintain moderate rate of speech when training in trainees' second language.

7. Find a local to be the translator of language and culture—someone who can step out of the trainee role and become the interpreter.

8. Train in the native language if possible—it helps empathy.

9. Use the written word and art graphics wherever possible.

10. Keep everything open for discussion.

Working with Interpreters

When trainers are not fluent in the language of the participant's country, they must overcome a linguistic barrier by using an interpreter.

Gary M. Wederspahn of MS&B International offers the following techniques and strategies for using interpreters that help reduce the risk of being misinterpreted and misunderstood:[25]

- Provide your interpreter with a written text or at least an outline of what you intend to communicate. In situations that require specialized or technical vocabulary, also provide a glossary of terms.

- Use professional interpreters. Effective translation is a demanding skill. Relying on bilingual colleagues to informally interpret in business dealings with outsiders may place unreasonable demands on them and lower their prestige in countries where the interpreter's role is one of low status. They may also make mistakes that a professional interpreter would not make.

- Both parties in a negotiation should employ their own interpreters. Depending entirely on a single interpreter places an unfair burden on that person. In addition, he or she will unconsciously represent the interests of his or her employee which may cause subtle changes in what you communicate and receive in return.

- Be aware of the interpreter's physical and emotional state (tiredness, hunger, stress, alcohol consumption, etc.). These factors may have a negative impact on the quality of the translation.

- Speak slowly and pronounce clearly. Limit your sentences to simple, short ones. Pause after each three or four sentences. Plan your presentation so that each group of sentences conveys a single topic or unit of the broader subject.

- Talk to the person with whom you are dealing, not to the interpreter. Maintain eye contact, if culturally appropriate, and convey interpersonal interest nonverbally.

- Avoid the use of slang, specialized sports terms, jargon, and idiomatic and colloquial expressions. Use standard English. Be aware of your own regional accent.

- Make use of charts, diagrams, photographs, outlines, and other visual aids. Often a single picture is worth a thousand words.

- If you choose to use metaphors, analogies, or literary allusions, be sure they are familiar to your listener and are commonly understood within the local cultural context.

- Beware of defective cognates. These are words that sound similar in both languages but have very different meanings. "Demander" in French, for example, means "ask" not "to demand." "Discuss" in English can be easily mistranslated in Spanish as "Discutir" which denotes dissension and argument.

- Do not use jokes or other attempts at humor. They rarely translate well and frequently result in bafflement at best and unintended insult at worst.

- Use specific quantifiable terms. Expressions that are, by nature, somewhat vague and imprecise such as "high quality" or "as soon as possible" are prone to cultural as well as linguistic misunderstanding. Specific terms will help avoid this problem.

- Carefully monitor the listener's facial expressions for signs of confusion. When in doubt regarding the clarity of the message received, ask for a reverse translation. This technique is a valuable, yet nonintrusive, check on accuracy.
- Practice using an interpreter before being in a situation of having to do so. Learning to use the previous skills and techniques requires time and effort.

Competencies for Global Trainers

Is the best U.S. trainer the best person to conduct training in other countries? Can any one person be familiar with all cultures and train in each one? Many questions arise around the issue of competencies for global trainers. There is concern about developing a competency model for global trainers. What could be perceived as a formula approach can lack depth or real understanding. So what competencies are needed by trainers to present global training?

Michael Paige of the University of Minnesota has researched the competencies trainers need to be effective in global training situations.[26] These competencies are listed in Figure 6–5.

Trainer Certification

Some corporations such as ASEA Brown Boveri (ABB) are designing trainer certification programs that ensure the quality of their training programs worldwide.[27] ABB has developed technical certification for its instructors. The next step in maintaining ABB Process Automation's leadership in training is to set training standards for its trainers and to certify their competence as training professionals.

ABB's research has identified the core skills needed by any professional trainer. These skills include the ability to:

- Present information clearly and effectively.
- Present information in a way meaningful to students, i.e., relate the new information to what the students already know.
- Use the basic principles of instructional design to modify and revise lessons to meet the needs of different student groups.
- Manage the learning of a group of students—maintaining the group's progress while still meeting the needs of individuals within the group.

- Recognize and clarify an individual student's need and respond appropriately.
- Coach individual students who may have special needs.

Technical trainers need yet another skill—that of simplifying complex information so it can be readily grasped by those who are less technically skilled. While trainers in a superior, worldwide training corporation can rely heavily on already designed, effective training materials, there are always occasions in which materials must be adapted to meet varying regional populations.

"Timely response to training needs is a critical factor in a global company," says Gordon Bennett, international training manager for ABB Process Automation.[28] Bennett knows that a quality organization must not only maintain quality standards, it must also do so quickly and with great flexibility. The marketplace is littered with failed companies that were unable to respond quickly enough to changing customer needs. A global corporation must be even more flexible as it works within a variety of cultures.

The selection and training of global trainers is fast emerging as a major factor in the success of multinational corporations. As we have seen in this chapter, companies must invest in a thorough selection process and an extensive training program for their human resource professionals. Effective global trainers must not only know training content and understand the technologies involved, but they must also have the added dimensions of multicultural awareness and specific cultural competence and experience. Only through a continuing education process can multinational companies truly compete in the global marketplace.

FIGURE 6–5
Competencies for the Global Trainer

Model 1:

Knowledge Area	*Knowledge Specifics*
Intercultural phenomena	1. Intercultural effectiveness, competence.
	2. Intercultural adjustment, culture shock.
	3. Reentry adjustment.
	4. Culture learning.
	5. The psychological and social dynamics of the intercultural experience.
Intercultural training	6. Training program assumptions: program philosophy, conceptual foundations of training, perspectives on learner needs, etc.
	7. Program planning principles: client needs assessment, audience analysis, staff training, logistics, timing, length, setting.
	8. Key training variables: audience diversity, trainer skills, length of program, predicted intensity of the intercultural experience, amount of affective and behavioral training.
	9. Realistic understanding of what training can and cannot accomplish.
	10. Realistic understanding of the relationship of training to performance in the target culture.
	11. Training design: goals and objectives, appropriate use of experiential and didactic methods, culture-specific and cultural-general content, cognitive/

(continued, next page)

FIGURE 6–5 *(continued)*

affective/behavioral learning, integrated training design that incorporates these elements.

12. Training pedagogy: appropriate selection and sequencing of learning activities, alternative training techniques, purposes of different activities, techniques for preparing culture learners (learning how to learn).

13. Program evaluation principles and methods.

Trainer-learner issues	14. Debriefing principles and strategies.
	15. The social psychological dynamics of the trainer-learner relationship: power, role modeling, risk of learner dependence on trainer.
	16. The nature and sources of learner resistance to training and potential learner reactions to intense training experiences: stress, anxiety, frustration, anger, resistance to training.
	17. Major learner concerns: threat to cultural identity, pressures to assimilate, challenge of becoming multicultural, becoming immobilized in a state of cultural relativism.
Ethical issues	18. Ethical issues in training: appropriate management of risks faced by learners (e.g., failure, self-disclosure); proper handling of the transformation imperative of training; creating a supportive rather than destructive learning environment.

(continued, next page)

FIGURE 6–5 *(continued)*

	19. The intercultural trainer's code of ethics.
Culture-specific content	20. The target culture: political, economic, social, cultural, demographic, religious, historical, and other factors.
	21. Situational factors in the target culture: host counterpart expectations, job clarity, openness to outsiders, host culture/ country relationship to own culture/ country, host culture/country aspirations.
	22. Values and attitudes of host culture.
	23. The nature of the occupational position: job roles and requirements.
Trainer issues	24. The role of the trainer in the learning process.
	25. The pressures that face trainers and methods for coping with them.
	26. One's own strengths and limitations as a trainer.
International issues	27. Theories of development, social change, transfer of technology.
	28. The issues of international relations: dependence versus interdependence, neo-colonialism, parity versus dominance.
Multicultural issues	29. Cultural pluralism and diversity: diversity and intercultural interactions in the workplace, society.
	30. The nature and impact of racism, sexism, and other forms of prejudice and discrimination.
	31. History of oppression and discrimination of groups being trained; history of inter-groups; relations of groups being trained.

(continued, next page)

FIGURE 6–5 *(continued)*

Model 2:

Behavioral Area	Behavioral Specifics
Intercultural phenomena	1. Capacity to promote learner acquisition of skills, knowledge, personal qualities relevant to intercultural effectiveness.
	2. Capacity to induce a cultural adjustment experience and to provide a culture-general conceptual framework to assist learners in coping with adjustment stresses.
	3. Capacity to conceptualize reentry issues and provide concrete ways for learners to maintain their connectedness with their home culture.
	4. Capacity to conceptualize the culture-learning phenomenon as a framework for thinking about intercultural experiences.
	5. Capacity to present theories and concepts regarding psychological and social dynamics of the intercultural experience: culture shock, intercultural communication and interaction, intercultural competence, etc.
Intercultural training	6. Ability to articulate a clear theory and research-based training philosophy and a statement of central training program assumptions.
	7. Ability to conduct planning activities, including staff training and development, needs analysis, audience assessment.
	8. Ability to effectively consider key training variables in program planning, design, and pedagogy.

(continued, next page)

FIGURE 6–5 (*continued*)

	9. Making appropriate claims for what training can and cannot accomplish.
	10. Making appropriate claims regarding the relationship of training to performance in the target culture.
	11. Ability to design integrated training programs having the appropriate mix of experiential and didactic methods, culture-specific and culture-general content, cognitive/affective/behavioral learning activities.
	12. Ability to implement an effective training pedagogy that effectively selects and sequences learning activities; uses alternative training techniques; clearly realizes the cognitive, affective, and behavioral purposes of different learning activities; and incorporates appropriate techniques of preparing culture learners (learning how to learn).
	13. Ability to conduct formative and summative program evaluations.
Trainer-learner issues	14. Ability to debrief learning activities with issues individuals and groups.
	15. Capacity to establish effective relationships with learners that reduce risk of learner dependence, minimize power and status differentials, build trust in the learning community.
	16. Capacity to help learners deal with stress, anxiety, frustration, etc.; ability to respond effectively and with sensitivity to learner resistance.
	17. Capacity to effectively treat difficult issues—cultural identity, assimilation,

(*continued, next page*)

FIGURE 6–5 *(continued)*

	multiculturalism, cultural relativism—in training design and pedagogy.
Ethical issues	18. Incorporation of ethical standards into all aspects of training.
	19. Firm adherence to the intercultural trainer's code of ethics, the ethical guidelines of the profession; this includes the willingness to improve one's own professional skills.
Culture-specific	20. Capacity to secure appropriate information and resources about the target culture: values, attitudes, politics, history, geography, etc.
	21. Capacity to assess situational factors in the field that will affect the work of the sojourner.
	22. Ability to assess and describe specific job roles, duties, and host counterpart expectations.
	23. Ability to provide instruction regarding target culture.
Trainer issues	24. Capacity to articulate, model, and orient learners to a clear philosophy of the trainer's role, to serve as a resource.
	25. Ability to handle the stress and pressures of training.
	26. Ability to conduct training activities in one's areas of strength; use of other skilled trainers for activities where one has more limited skills.
International issues	27. Ability to present theories of development, social change, transfer of technology.

(continued, next page)

FIGURE 6–5 (*continued*)

	28. Ability to engage learners in thinking about the central issues of international relations, especially as these will affect them personally; dependence versus interdependence, impact of the colonial legacy, parity versus dominance or superiority.
Multicultural issues	29. Capacity to instruct about cultural pluralism and diversity: intercultural interactions in the workplace, society.
	30. Capacity to provide consciousness-raising education about the nature and impact of racism, sexism, and other forms of prejudice and discrimination.
	31. Capacity to design training programs that are sensitive to the history of oppression, discrimination, and intergroup relations of the groups being trained.
	32. Capacity to conceptualize and provide supportive social and psychological mechanisms for dealing with cultural marginality and multiculturalism.

(*continued, next page*)

FIGURE 6–5 (*concluded*)

Model 3:

Trainer Competencies: Personal Attributes

1. Tolerance of ambiguity
2. Cognitive and behavioral flexibility
3. Personal self-awareness, strong personal identity
4. Cultural self-awareness
5. Patience
6. Enthusiasm and commitment
7. Interpersonal sensitivity, relations
8. Tolerance of differences
9. Openness to new experiences, people
10. Empathy
11. Sense of humility
12. Sense of humor

Source: "Trainer Competencies for International and Intercultural Programs," in R. Michael Paige, ed., *Education for the Intercultural Experience*, Intercultural Press, Inc.,1993.

Chapter Seven

Managing a Multinational Training System

The world is my country and all mankind are my brethren.

—Thomas Paine

Think globally...act locally has become the call to action for multinational corporations. As more U.S. corporations move into the global arena, they must, on the one hand, continue to compete at home in what has been the world's largest single market and, at the same time, develop a global mindset to win in world markets.[1] In 1988, General Electric (GE) began applying action learning with a global perspective in its training programs. Currently, all of GE's executive education programs are worldwide in scope. This focus is in line with GE's strategic goal for each of its 13 businesses to be first or second in the global market. The corporate training management system must also embrace both domestic and global markets and provide appropriate training for employees worldwide.

Nancy Adler and Susan Bartholomew point out that, in global human resource management "The clear issue is that strategy (the *what*) is internationalizing faster than implementation (the *how*) and much faster than individual managers and executives themselves (the *who*)."[2] Human resource management for the global firm includes both personnel and training issues. Designing and implementing global performance appraisal systems and the benefits, compensation, and rewards for worldwide employees is a tremendous challenge. The focus for this chapter, however, is on educating company employees through a global training system.

The multifaceted task of establishing and managing a firm's global training program can be overwhelming at best. Not only have most training managers had little international experience, they are also faced with the everchanging global workforce and markets as well. In earlier chapters, the foundation for the global training function was discussed. The basic steps in developing the program are:

1. Assess your company employees to discover who needs global training and what training they need.
2. Assist top-level managers and executives in developing a global mindset.
3. Create a global training strategy and tie it in with the corporate strategy.
4. Design guidelines for producing multinational training courses.
5. Develop a global training curriculum.
6. Select carefully and provide training for trainers and human resource staff.

AMERICAN SOCIETY FOR TRAINING AND DEVELOPMENT (ASTD) TASK FORCE

In 1991, an ASTD Task Force on global training issues met in San Francisco. These experienced global human resource managers and multinational consultants were asked, "What advice would you give to executives who manage international training programs?" They identified five areas in managing the multinational training process: develop a global focus, operate regionally, understand local government regulations, build training alliances, and determine worldwide costs. The comments from the Task Force include the following suggestions.

I. Develop a global focus.
   A. Champion employee individuality and cross-cultural differences.
   B. Adapt to your company's changing markets.
   C. Be proactive and flexible.
   D. Plan for the future.

II. Operate Regionally.
   A. Obtain input and investment from all organizational levels. Local, regional, and subsidiary offices should be authorized to initiate training programs.

B. Study how regional training centers and other large-scale experiments are designed and managed in countries outside the United States.

C. Align what you are trying to achieve with the nature of your clients. Training managers in a new country must understand both corporate values and cultural values.

D. Demonstrate a corporate willingness to embrace the idea of cooperation with local management.

E. Establish a training advisory counsel at international sites with managers from the local area to help them break away from a dependence on the United States—let them determine training and build their own training programs appropriate to that setting.

F. Emphasize that the relationship between American-based trainers and local site trainers must be a relationship of equals.

G. Consider three factors when designing training for another country: the local culture's language, the local citizens' perspective on appropriate content, and how they view supervision, roles, and responsibility.

III. Understand local government regulations.

A. Learn the specific laws and customs that regulate your company's business in that country and, more specifically, how these regulations affect training employees locally.

B. Meet government officials and discuss how you can work together within their customs. Since most countries are eager for more education for their nationals, tap into this interest by opening up a dialogue on training. Investigate how the training your company presents can meet the educational objectives for the country as well.

IV. Build training alliances.

A. Strengthen multicultural teambuilding.

B. Understand that a training consultant can often become your company's global leader, helping employees make decisions with sensitivity to cultural issues.

C. When you are under the gun to quickly put a training program in place at an overseas site.

1. Use local academic resources, such as universities or community colleges for guidance, suggestions, and insight.

2. Spend time with the end users of training to find out what they need and want.

3. Work with internal or external clients to define their goals for the training. In other words, start with the end result and then design the training course to produce the desired results.
4. Understand the way the participant audience learns best.
5. Make the line manager a central member of the team.
6. Identify local people who can present the training.
V. Determine costs.
   A. Realize up front that training costs increase as you expand globally.
   B. Obtain budget information from other global corporations, international consulting firms, and local managers who have experience in this area.

These suggestions are important for the training director who is new to the global training process and for more experienced global training managers as well. Let's now look at a more detailed discussion of these five global training management areas.

DEVELOP A GLOBAL FOCUS

ASEA Brown Bovier (ABB) is a global company cited in both the *Harvard Business Review* and *Fortune* as a successful multinational firm. In the last few years, CEO Percy Barnevik has led the march in creating this globally focused corporation. By merging ASEA, a Swedish engineering group, to Brown Boveri, a Swiss competitor, and adding 70 more companies across Europe and the United States, he has created this worldwide leader in high-speed trains, robotics, and environmental control. Barnevik has chosen only 250 global managers to oversee ABB's 210,000 employees.

Although ABB's corporate headquarters are in Zurich, the 13 top executives hold meetings frequently in various countries. Barnevik supports the belief that the best strategy is to break free of protected national markets and become totally global. "The companies that we have bought in the United States are so focused on the American market that we have to help them think about the rest of the world. We add the global dimension they lack," he states.[3] An effective global manager, according to Barnevik, has patience, good language ability, stamina, work experience in at least two or three countries and, most important, humility. Commitment to the corporation is another important factor for ABB top managers since they are expected to put in long hours. These managers often add 30 hours a week to their regular work schedules to incorporate travel, attending conferences, and evening seminars.

Expand the Training Process

While firms have formulated corporate strategies to meet new global challenges, most of them are not capable of implementing the strategies they have created. Even after global training mission statements and training strategies are developed, current domestic training systems do not have the capacity to make these plans operational. To achieve global scope, training managers must expand their process to meet the corporation's worldwide market. One of the ways to build this global training system is to gather information on what other multinational firms are doing. Companies benchmark their corporate performance against best practices in other firms. Similarly, training managers must identify superior training standards in other global organizations.

Develop a Corporatewide Pool of Global Trainers

Some multinational corporations have developed a global training strategy in which they establish and maintain a corporatewide pool of global trainers who are available for international assignments. Experienced managers from this cadre are not only available for other global positions but are often targeted by the company in the executive succession planning process. For example, Philips' corporate pool consists of employees from more than 50 nationalities. Each individual has at least five years of experience and is ranked in the top 20 percent on performance.[4]

These trainers are not placed in any one physical location but become members of this special group because they have developed the ability to share information and work with employees from many different countries and cultures. Then, as regional training operations are established in various geographic areas, these identified multinational trainers are prepared to train employees in new regional centers or to design a training course for that location.

OPERATE REGIONALLY

More corporate human resource executives are setting up training management teams in regions around the world. Often housed within a manufacturing facility, these training centers are accessible for training support to employees at that plant site and to marketing, sales, customer service, and other company employees located in that geographic region. The training staff in these regional centers may be from the host country or from the firm's training pool of experienced global trainers. The staff's mission is to train employees in each region not only to perform successfully in their current jobs at that location but to also prepare them eventually to work on culturally diverse teams anywhere in the world.

Arranging Culturally Diverse Training

Training executives are discovering that cultural diversity can indeed become a valuable resource if it is managed competently. Culturally diverse global training teams can provide a wider range of approaches and can increase creativity and flexibility in the training process. Not only are company training teams becoming more multicultural, but participant mix is increasingly international as well. Many global corporations are sending U.S. employees to training courses around the world. They are also transporting non-U.S. employees to corporate headquarters to participate in training in an American setting. This plan provides not only the needed training, but a cross-cultural experience as well. Movement across borders can increase the employee globalization process for the corporation.

Two corporations who use such a global approach are Ericsson and Olivetti. Each company created a management development center in which both the staff and participants come from all regions of the world. To minimize the possibility of headquarters' cultural dominance, each company located its management development center in a more culturally neutral country rather than at their headquarters' location (Ericsson—Sweden and Olivetti— Italy).[5]

Selecting a Training Advisory Council

Multinational corporations often use managers outside the company as advisers in the local area. For example, Amoco developed a European Training Advisory Counsel selecting managers from the local area to help them break away from a dependence on U.S.-determined training and to build their own training programs appropriate to that local setting.[6]

Motorola uses regional training boards composed of all the senior executives of that region to direct the training program. It has regional boards for Asia, Europe, and for various regions in the United States. In 1985, only 25 percent of Motorola's sales came from outside the United States With major operations located in Asia, Japan, Europe, Canada, South America, and the United States, global sales by 1991 had risen to 50 percent of total sales. In 1988, as Asia Pacific director of training, K. L. Cheah was responsible for the training and education of 22,000 Motorola employees and assisted in the design of Motorola's Singapore Training Center. "The main mission of the Singapore Training Center is to design and deliver training programs both for the corporation and for the government of Singapore," says Cheah, the current director for planning at Motorola University.[7]

Establishing Regional Training Centers

Motorola's Singapore Training Center also formed an alliance with the Singapore government to develop customized training, including a train-the-trainer course, for the people of Singapore. Cheah states, "We designed a 300-hour instructional design diploma for them. Not only do we customize programs that are appropriate for their culture, but we also teach them how to design other programs. So it is a win-win situation for us. We are able to experiment and work on understanding their culture in the design process, as we provide these customized training programs for the Singapore government." Currently, Motorola partners with 17 universities worldwide in Europe, Asia, and the United States. The Singapore Training Center forms partnerships with local universities so they can help with the training content and design. In return, Motorola shares design technology and programs with faculty there.

European Director of Training Albert Scius was sent by Coulter Corporation, an international biomedical firm based in Florida, to investigate setting up a regional training center in Europe. Although the primary objective of most regional training centers is designing training for employees, other motives are also evident. "Part of the rationale for establishing this center is that we want to be closer to our customers and our markets," Scius explains.[8] The center also can be an effective communication channel. Crossing time zones can create barriers to communication flow. "The manager at corporate headquarters must realize that the employee calling from France has to wake up in the middle of the night to meet a phone deadline in Miami, Florida. So language and cultural differences are not the only communication factors," Scius says. A regional training center can provide prompt communication and feedback and help ensure that company messages are received and understood. Another obvious reason for establishing regional training centers is to avoid duplication. The company must have a consistent product presentation to convey the same message to its customers worldwide. Because of modern technology it's a very small world, and consistency is important. Also, increased motivation and productivity are biproducts of these training centers as regional training managers provide coaching in addition to more formal training.

Scius has several important tips on global training logistics to pass along to training managers operating courses in regional training centers:

- When you are in a new area, be sure to identify an ally in that country, someone you can trust and talk with directly. The ally can provide feedback on what is appropriate or not appropriate.

- If the trainers do not speak the language fluently, have them learn key words. The participants will be pleased if the trainers can at least say good morning and thank you in the host-country language. This courtesy opens participants' minds and makes them more receptive in the training sessions.

- Ship any training material prior to arrival. Deliveries may be delayed, and conducting training without the necessary tools can be ineffective. Send the material early so the local managers can review it. The trainer will get early buy-in and can work with the local staff to reproduce the handouts.

- Be sure the electrical equipment uses the same electrical current that is available in the host country's facilities. Review the media and make sure that the content is appropriate in the country's national culture. Be cognizant that an excellent video in one country may not work in another. Trainers must be careful not to offend the participants. Use the country contact and have him or her review all the material. The trainer should plan to have at least one day free to check equipment and materials before the training begins.

- Keep your promises. If you want to continue training efforts in that country, keep your promises or otherwise lose your credibility. Ask for feedback after the training session, but be sure you do this in an appropriate way.

UNDERSTAND LOCAL
GOVERNMENT REGULATIONS

To be successful in multinational markets, the global corporation must understand government procedures and the legal issues of conducting business in each country. The mere act of dealing with a different government can be an immensely eye-opening experience. The corporation and the government both have needs, and sometimes those needs are in direct conflict. Knowing the government regulations and customs is an important factor in developing a company's global training management system. Steve Ginsburgh, manager of organizational services and employee development for Maxus Energy Corporation, explains the working relationships in an international location in Figure 7–1. To accomplish training goals in a specific nation, the working dynamics between the corporation, government, national employees, and expatriate managers must be communicated and understood.

"Basically, it's a control issue. The corporation would like to control what it has, and the government would like to gain more control in this partnership that the corporation has arranged in its country," says Ginsburgh.[9]

Discussing Business Ethics

Discussing business ethics in culturally diverse groups is a volatile issue. Customary ways of doing business in one country may be viewed as unethical or illegal in another country. A corporation's legal staff can be of tremendous help with training in this regulatory area. The staff can provide information on what is legal and what is illegal for a specific country's business practices. "For example, training is often driven by the government's requirements that, as of a certain date, your operation will be nationalized. That means you have to train a national staff that will run it and then move your expatriates out of the country," Ginsburgh states.

Conducting Business Outside the United States

Lawrence Tuller's book, *Going Global*, provides a wealth of general information on conducting business in other countries.[10] Although the information in the book is not always country specific, Tuller covers important details for doing business outside the United States. His suggestions on how to get through customs in a third-world country, how to staff an office in another country, and the basics of import/export issues can prove helpful to businesses and training managers working globally.

BUILD TRAINING ALLIANCES

Corporations are realizing that competing globally today can best be accomplished through partnering and collaboration. Training managers also can profit from building alliances with local training resources throughout the world.

FIGURE 7–1
Players Who Influence the Training Process

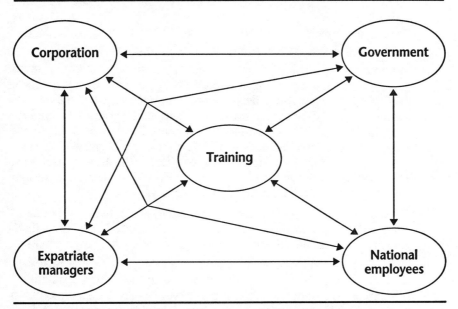

Source: Steve Ginsburgh, manager of organizational services and employee development, Maxus Energy Corporation. Presentation at ASTD pre-conference workshop, New Orleans, LA, May 1992.

William D. Shea, director of the Center for Creative Leadership's European office, believes that "Anyone who doubts we have a lot to learn from our colleagues overseas should never leave the United States. In my first two years in Brussels, I learned much more than I could ever teach. Peter Drucker is right when he says, 'Managers do the same thing all over the world; the *way* they do it is different'." [11]

Forming Training Alliances

In addition to building alliances with universities, governments, and local leaders, Shea sees several other types of training alliances available in the global arena:

- Licensing. This is a common practice within the United States that is spreading internationally. Training vendors who have developed success-ful programs on a variety of training topics provide training certification so trainers can present their programs within companies. The vendor or consulting firm charges a licensing fee and usually sells participant and instructor materials to the company. Some consulting firms are translating their training programs into other languages, such as Spanish, German, French, and Japanese, and also are adapting them to the specific culture. Licensing is an easy way to access and obtain a training program.

- Subcontracting. Sometimes a company subsidiary or government needs a training program delivered for its employees and does not have the time or the expertise to design a program internally. It can then subcontract a consulting firm to design and present the course for employees. This type of contract is also viable when a U.S. consulting firm has a client corporation that needs a training course in a country whose language and culture is outside the experience of the U.S. consultants. They, in turn, may subcontract to a local consulting business to design and present the training for the client company.

- Co-contracting. Co-contracting is a process in which two or more training organizations work on an equal basis on a training project. Each partnering firm in the alliance brings its strengths to the design process.

- Co-design and delivery. This method of training design is a relatively recent type of alliance especially applicable to international situations. It is similar to co-contracting except the partners are trainers internal to the company and an external consulting firm. The company has firsthand knowledge of the employees, the industry, the language, and the country's culture. It is involved as an equal partner with the consulting firm which contributes expertise in the training topic and process. This equal sharing by both parties not only produces a more effective training product, it also promotes an on-the-job type learning experience for both organizations.

Rather than spend time and money on start-ups, corporations are learning to focus more on their areas of expertise and to partner with other companies for expanded capabilities. Training managers can also use this idea to their advantage. Alliance building lets corporate training managers concentrate on their objectives and what they do best. At the same time, they are able to tap into the expertise they do not have and learn from others. "Ultimately, the survival of mankind will depend upon the ability to think together and act together, to think differently and still act together," Shea said. Cultural awareness is as essential in alliance building as it is within the corporate workforce. Training executives must not only promote multicultural awareness, they must understand and manage diversity both internally and externally as one of their most valuable resources.

Selecting Global Consultants

Corporations are using external consultants for most of their cross-cultural needs. Since multiculturalism is sometimes an unfamiliar area for training managers, selection guidelines can prove helpful. Gary M. Wederspahn, director of program design and development for Moran, Stahl, & Boyer International's division, suggests some specific criteria:[12]

- Multiple referrals. Obtain the names and telephone numbers of at least three clients and contact them directly.

- The International Society for Intercultural Education, Training, and Research (SIETAR) leadership. Consult the professional society for cross-cultural trainers, researchers, and educators, SIETAR, 808 17th Street, N.W., Suite 200, Washington, DC 20006, (202) 466-7883. Remember, membership alone is not evidence of expertise, as the society is open to virtually anyone. However, those who are regularly asked to make presentations at the annual conferences are basically the acknowledged leaders in the field.

- Organizational stability. Look for a serious, stable consultant who has been in the business continuously for at least five years. Groups form and disband and individual practitioners enter and leave the field with alarming frequency.

- Organizational depth. Know the number of professionals and associates in the consulting firm to help determine project availability.

- Organizational breadth. Ask consultants about the number of countries in which they have conducted training and how many different services they offer.

- Client responsiveness. Look for responsiveness and commitment to adapting the consultants' model and approach as necessary.

- Appropriate experience. Seek evidence of corporate experience and involvement with multinational firms on serious international business projects.

- Pragmatic focus. Request written objectives for proposed programs and evaluate them against your own criteria for useful, tangible skills and insights.

- Active learning. Determine that the consultants use participative involvement and active learning in their training sessions.

- Ongoing research and development. Look for evidence that the consultant is actively involved in ongoing research and development.

- In-house talent. Find out if the consultants' major talent and creativity belong to their own organization or if they rely exclusively on the ideas and work of others.
- Quality assurance. Determine if past programs and services have been formally evaluated by the participants. Were evaluation reports given to clients? Were follow-up evaluations done? Ask for copies.
- Human warmth. Assess the level of interest in people on the part of the potential supplier's training staff. Assisting expatriate families through difficult adjustment challenges requires genuine caring.

DETERMINE COSTS

One of the more frustrating areas of training management is the budget area. Not only do training directors have difficulty determining costs, they usually are even more hard pressed to obtain the budget necessary to provide adequate employee training. In the global arena, training executives may be overwhelmed because of their lack of experience at providing training worldwide.

Michael J. Copeland of Procter & Gamble's international division explains that global training time and costs are usually higher because of the language and cultural differences between the United States and the host country. He suggests that costs, depending on the scope of the differences, are often double the cost of training employees within the United States.[13]

The training manager must carefully analyze the overall costs and time variables to be sure they are estimated correctly. Variables include the training location, time needed for training design and delivery, travel expenses for the trainer and family, medical insurance and other benefits, and incidental expenses to be paid by the company. Copeland warns that the cost of relocating employees and their families can be twice their usual salary and benefits. Other factors that have budget implications are the tax laws and the currency rates of both countries.

Some of this information may be obtained from internal company resources. If the figures are not available, the human resource manager can gather information from peers in other transnational corporations. Experienced global managers can explain their costs and procedures. Also the National Foreign Trade Council, American Council on International Personnel, the National Association of Manufacturers, or other such organizations can act as referral agencies to assist in finding the correct information.

MEETING THE GLOBAL CHALLENGE

Christopher A. Bartlett and Sumantra Ghosal identify three roles at the core of the global manager's job: a global strategist, an architect of the company's worldwide asset and resource configuration, and a coordinator of activities across national borders.[14] These roles—strategist, architect, and coordinator—are also the overriding responsibility of the global training manager.

As discussed in this chapter, establishing and managing a global training system involves:

I. Developing a global focus.
   A. Expanding the training process.
   B. Developing a corporatewide pool of global trainers.

II. Operating regionally.
   A. Arranging culturally diverse training.
   B. Selecting a training advisory council.
   C. Establishing regional training centers.

III. Understanding local government regulations.
   A. Discussing business ethics.
   B. Conducting business outside the United States.

IV. Building training alliances.
   A. Forming training alliances.
   B. Selecting global consultants.

V. Determining budget costs.

The steps in setting up a global training program outlined in this book are:

1. Assess global training needs.

2. Assist management to think globally.

3. Create a global training strategy.

4. Design and follow guidelines for multinational training.

5. Develop a global training curriculum.

6 Select and train global trainers.

7. Manage the multinational training system.

Perhaps, the primary function of global human resource executives, however, is to remain open to change and to encourage the openness and experimentation needed to create truly global systems. Unless the training management system is globally focused and supports the corporate business strategy, the global firm cannot succeed. Global training managers need to discard traditional models and begin to think from a global rather than a domestic paradigm. The next few years will be critical in determining how well companies, industries, and countries meet the challenge of competition in a worldwide marketplace. Effective training can be the secret weapon that helps *your* company succeed where others merely survive...or fail.

Training Resources

FILMS

Going International is a series of four films that help orient Americans to cultural differences around the world:

- *Bridging the Culture Gap.*
- *Managing the Overseas Assignment.*
- *Beyond Culture Shock.*
- *Welcome Home Stranger.*

Films for non-U.S. citizens:

- *Working in the U.S.A.*
- *Living in the U.S.A.*

Film for all travelers:

- *Going International—Safely.*

Each film title has a user's guide for participants that expands upon the film and provides exercises, checklists, and additional resources. Produced and distributed by:

    Griggs Productions
    302 23rd Avenue
    San Francisco, CA 94121
    (415) 668-4200

Tearing Down the Walls: The GEO Changing Forces is a video about three areas of change: globalization, empowerment, and orchestration. The video package includes a leader's guide, a mind map, and a GEO grid. Produced and distributed by:

> The GEO Group, Inc.
> 5405 Alton Parkway
> Irvine, CA 92714
> (714) 851-6555

Bridges: Skills for Managing a Diverse Workforce features eight video-based modules each addressing a different diversity issue:

- *Intercultural Perceptions.*
- *Gender Stereotypes.*
- *Subtle Racial Stereotypes.*
- *Ethnic Identity/Organizational Culture.*
- *Cultural "In" Groups/ "Out" Groups.*
- *Intercultural Conflicts.*
- *Culture/Gender Stereotypes.*
- *Communication Barriers.*

Videos are complete with trainers' manuals and participants' manuals. Produced and distributed by:

> BNA Communications Inc.
> 9439 Key West Avenue
> Rockville, MD 20850
> (800) 233-6067

Doing Business Internationally—The Cross-Cultural Challenges is a video training package designed to enable managers to develop the skills and attitudes required for effective international management and to provide an in-depth analysis of the impact of culture on business practices. Combining graphics, live action, and interviews with international management consultant Stephen Rhinesmith and executives from Colgate-Palmolive, Ernst & Young, and AT&T, the video covers:

- *Internationalization*
- *What is Culture?*

- *Culture and International Negotiation*
- *Culture and International Management*
- *Culture and International Marketing*
- *Conclusion—The International Manager*

The 43-minute video is accompanied by a leader's guide, participant's workbook, and an audio cassette.
Produced and distributed by:
MultiMedia Inc.
15 North Summit Street
Tenafly, NJ 07670
(800) 682-1992

Living and Working in America is a three-volume video/audio series specially designed to help workers who are new to American culture improve their language and socialization skills. Serious communication problems can arise from the anxiety, isolation, and frustration nonnative speakers often feel. They need training which specifically addresses the linguistic and cultural needs of nonnative English speakers who are adjusting to working with Americans. This multi-media program includes video and audio tapes, textbook, and instructor's manual.
Produced and distributed by:
VIA Press, Inc.
400 E. Evergreen Blvd., Suite 314
Vancouver, WA 98660
(800) 944-8421

COUNTRY-SPECIFIC INFORMATION

- The U.S. Department of State, Bureau of Public Affairs, Office of Public Communication provides *Country Profiles and Background Notes* that are sold through the:
Superintendent of Documents
U.S. Government Printing Office
Washington, DC 20402-9324
(202) 783-3238

- **Culturgrams** provide clear, concise information about the daily lives of people in more than 100 areas of the world.

Culturgrams
P. O. Box 10777
Golden, CO 80401-0610
(800) 528-6279

Nonprofit Organizations:
Brigham Young University
Kennedy Center Publications
280 HRCB
Provo, UT 84602
(801) 378-6528

- *Cultural Diversity at Work* is published in six bimonthly newsletters and 11 monthly bulletins by:
  The Gildeane Group
  13751 Lake City Way N.E., Suite 106
  Seattle, WA 98125-3615
  (206) 362-0336

- **Intercultural Press** publishes global and multicultural books.
  Intercultural Press, Inc.
  P. O. Box 700
  Yarmouth, ME 04096
  (207) 846-5168

ORGANIZATIONS

- **American Society for Training and Development (ASTD)**
  International Professional Practice Area
  1640 King Street
  Box 1443
  Alexandria, VA 22313-2043
  (703) 683-8100

- **The International Society for Intercultural Education, Training and Research (SIETAR International)**
  808 17th Street, N.W., Suite 200
  Washington, DC 20006
  (202) 466-7883

- **The Multicultural Institute of the International Counseling Center**
  3000 Connecticut Avenue, NW, Suite 138
  Washington, DC 20008
  (202) 483-0700

- **Society for Human Resource Management (SHRM)**
  Institute for International Human Resources
  606 N. Washington Street
  Alexandria, VA 22314
  (703) 548-3440

Case Study: Start-up of a Global Training Program

B ill Matheny, former corporate manager of training and development for Hogan Systems, Inc., provides this case study of the start-up of a global training program for a multinational financial software company.

BACKGROUND

Hogan Systems produces mainframe software solutions and provides consulting services to large banks and financial institutions worldwide. The company was nearly 13 years old but was still operating in an entrepreneurial mode and had not implemented a policy of employee development beyond providing for some tuition reimbursement for college coursework.

Although the firm employed less than 500 professionals, it maintained two European offices and an office in the South Pacific. Consultants representing many nationalities were pulled together on a project at a client location. The team's objective was to provide various product installations and service over time periods from two months to three years. Matheny used four phases in developing and implementing this global training program: assess and plan strategy, develop training models, design or buy training, and implement in multinational/multicultural environments.

PHASE I: ASSESS AND PLAN STRATEGY

The first order of business is to assess and understand the firm and the employees' training needs. This is true of any training start-up, but the major difference in this case—and it was major—was the company's multinational operation and the complexity of its product service. The basic steps to follow in Phase I are:

- Conduct a needs assessment.
- Collect education and training data on all employees.
- Survey client requirements.
- Create or revise policies.
- Write or revise job descriptions.
- Conduct employee opinion surveys.
- Interview corporate executives.

Policy issues are often ignored in U.S. companies where training and education are concerned. When developing a strategy for multinational environments, policy issues must be given early attention. Policies and procedures can enhance implementation with quality and consistency in mind. Some of the policies to be developed include:

- Education tuition reimbursement—some cultures may even demand a 100 percent coverage for their employees.
- Specific job training for all classified functions listed as job descriptions.
- Safety and environmental issues.
- Community responsibility in the area of training and education. This could be in the form of donations, classes, and general support for economic and social enhancements.
- Local and regional professional membership affiliations.

All of the listed areas should have a policy that can accommodate that country's cultural expectations and go beyond those expectations when existing conditions show less than productive growth and satisfactory profits.

PHASE II: DEVELOP TRAINING MODELS

Training models must be developed for job functions. All functions should be analyzed in terms of multinational, cross-cultural, and multicultural considerations. Considerations must also be given to the type of employee assigned to various functions and how that function applies to the specific business and client base. Activities during this phase and how to implement them are:

- Develop training models for each significant function (i.e., sulting, marketing).
- Note similarities and differences in the models to enable leveraging with course selection.
- Consider delivery methods and location as they apply to your specific business and employee composition. All options are open for delivery even though they may not always be feasible.

PHASE III: DESIGN OR BUY TRAINING

Two of the foremost considerations in identifying and planning specific training courses are cost considerations and available resources. These factors influence the decision to design, buy, or use a combined approach. In a domestic operation you need to consider those resources available in the United States. In training non-U.S. employees, however, you must also consider global resources. In Phase III you should:

- Review your internal development capability.
- Purchase off-the-shelf training programs if appropriate.
- Interview consultants and purchase custom-designed training programs from selected consultants.
- Review materials and providers in countries where training is needed or from providers in countries who are known to be good resources.

In developing training for a non-U.S. country, it is important to use designers who are familiar with the culture and training processes in that country. Buying off-the-shelf programs should be given the same considerations. Use vendors and consultants who have multinational experience and can assist you with your training needs. Often, budgets do not reflect the unique cost associated with presenting training in a multinational setting. This needs to be addressed early in your process.

Products purchased must be available through licenses outside the United States, and in some cases, in other languages. Product quality is a concern. In some cases, it may be necessary to review materials produced by vendors in the host country, especially if cultural considerations are an issue. You may need to wade through this one on a case-by-case basis. Once you know other markets and make contacts for evaluation, this will be a more pleasant activity.

On three occasions, internal development was necessary, either because the external courses were unavailable or because of specific content requirements. The three occasions were:

1. Performance appraisal training for managers and supervisors.
2. A multinational recruiting and interviewing workshop.
3. Consultant training for company consultants working in a variety of environments and cultures.

When considering a design-or-buy situation for multinational training, objectivity is very important. Problems can be compounded in an international setting when options for midcourse correction and implementation strategies are just not possible. The key is to involve the client in the initial decision process. This is true for internal as well as external clients.

PHASE IV: IMPLEMENT IN MULTINATIONAL/ MULTICULTURAL ENVIRONMENTS

The following considerations are important for Phase IV:

- Use local talent whenever possible for delivery.
- Train and prepare trainers who have not had a multicultural training experience.
- Resolve logistics issues well in advance of the training activity.
- Be sensitive to workplace relationships that can be a source of conflict.
- Be patient, tolerant, and aware of how you represent your company or home office.
- Be aware of how you represent your profession.
- From a methodology and delivery standpoint, learn what works best within a given culture (i.e., role playing, high structure, lecture, games, video).

Some of the more obvious logistics, but definitely not the least difficult to overcome, are items like shipping materials, transporting photos, videotapes, and customs problems.

Remember that you are a visitor to someone else's company, country, and culture. Do not try to impose your values and practices on them. Many corporations and businesses are becoming more conscious of cultural diversity.

However, this does not mean that the same companies are multicultural in practice. Walking the talk is required here.

Specific training courses selected for Hogan Systems were:

- Business technology and services for the banking and financial industry.
- Specific company product training.
- Time and project management.
    —Project management part I—Administration.
    —Project management part II—Software for Project Management.
- Leadership and teamwork.
- Consultant training for new and experienced consultants.
- Supervisory and management training.
- Presentation skills.
- Multicultural management.

Employees targeted for training were consultants, project managers, and sales representatives and their support staff. Courses were delivered on location at a client's facility anywhere in the world. Sequencing always presents a problem, so it was necessary to plan training to benefit the consultant team as a unit first and for individuals second. This provided more leverage with both the client and home office managers.

Here are some tips that can prove helpful for the global training manager:

- Review the material that's produced in a host country. This is a professional courtesy. If you're working with a client outside of your own environment, then involve the client. Talk to any particular vendor the client has used in the past and about successes and failures with the host-country material.
- Produce case studies and exercises that relate to the host country's cultural situations.
- Join several national and multinational training organizations.
- Develop a network of organizations to handle both language and multicultural and diversity issues. Hogan Systems operates in 42 countries, so developing a network is an important factor in setting up a global training program.

Appendix C

Using Active Participation Training in Kuwait

Taken from *The Herald*, Corporate Learning Institute, Vanderbilt University, August 24, 1992

How do you walk the walk without stepping on any toes? This was the challenge that Kurt Weiss and Janet Eyler of Vanderbilt's Corporate Learning Institute (CLI) faced as they prepared to spend two weeks working with the training staff of the Kuwait Institute for Scientific Research (KISR) in February 1992. They knew that the Middle East, like most nonwestern cultures, has strong nonconfrontational norms. The personal risk taking and public feedback so central to the view of CLI on participative learning were potentially dangerous territory in a Kuwaiti classroom.

Many resources they consulted advised starting slowly by using lecture and other passive techniques more typical of instruction in that part of the world and then easing into more active involvement with participants. However, Weiss and Eyler were unwilling to make this compromise which they felt would undercut the credibility of what they had to offer. They were determined to adapt the program to respect the local culture as well as the adult learning process. This involved some careful planning so that they could plunge right into active participation while making sure the participants were comfortable with the process. Part of their success was evident the first day, when participants insisted on converting the classroom from rows of armchairs with notepads for lectures to tables and chairs where their teams could work more comfortably.

Weiss and Eyler used a four-pronged strategy:

1. They chose a coherent design model with a heavy feedback component (Critical Events Model) as the skeleton for the course. With this

model, participants could always see where they were going and how current activities fit into the plan.

2. They made the plan flexible with removable, expandable and repeatable modules so that they could adapt to the needs that emerged. This made adapting to the many changes in scheduling that faced them relatively easy.

3. They customized the materials to include culturally appropriate pictures in the visuals and names in the case and role-play material. They also used learner experience to customize the training. They were the experts on the design and evaluation techniques participants in the Kuwait training wanted to learn. Participants were the experts on the needs of their institute and the cultural norms that trainers in their country needed to observe. Many lessons involved their expertise in adapting processes to appropriate local practice. "We truly learned as much from them as they did from us," said Eyler.

4. They planned and emphasized multiple opportunities for safe participation early in the workshop. By the end of the first day, participants had:
   a. Been involved in a participative object lesson and brainstorming.
   b. Taken part in interviews and introductions.
   c. Critiqued a bad example role play by the trainers.
   d. Identified trends within Kuwait that influence human resource development needs.
   e. Created their own model of Kuwait adult learning.
   f. Worked in teams on a case study.

All of these activities involved everyone in the process without the risk of wrong answers or public loss of face. Once this safe climate was established, many participants were willing to take more risks. As the workshop progressed, discussions became more open, and real institute problems could be dealt with as part of the learning process.

While Weiss and Eyler were impressed by the teams' performance on an all-day design simulation, the high point for them came in the closing activity when the group was asked to replay the roles that they had performed as a bad example the first morning. The group clustered in the middle of the room and spent 20 minutes speaking in rapid Arabic. Two participants then played an *ideal* consultation between the chief executive officer and director of training, blending the information and skills they had acquired about human resource development during the two weeks together with a conversational style appropriate to the positions they were playing within their culture. "It was excellent, and exactly what we had hoped for!" Eyler concluded.

—By Janet Eyler

Appendix D

OrgSim™—A Simulated Global Organization

Dr. Kenneth L. Murrell and
BJ Chakiris, 1992

THE NATURE OF THE SIMULATION

The Organization is a learning-based simulation; that is, it is designed to simulate the experiences of individuals in any organization. The learnings of participants from their involvement in the game can be applied to all kinds of organizations: businesses (for-profit organizations), as well as not-for-profit organizations, such as volunteer groups, governmental agencies, associations and educational organizations such as universities or public school districts.

As a participant in The Organization, you are expected to try to realize your personal and professional life goals, whatever those may be. As you work with others in the group who have their own goals, you will discover some of the possibilities and limits on your own behavior.

As a simulation, The Organization will not replicate every aspect of organizational life. No simulation can copy every aspect of everyday life. However, its purpose is to reduplicate the most salient and important facets of what we all experience in normal participation in organizations.

On the other hand, every group that creates its own organization creates something unique, for the nature of each group's organization will depend on the individual goals of all the participants and how those interact with one another.

The purpose of the simulation, again, is to provide you with a learning experience. It gives you an opportunity to experiment with new behaviors, learn from your current behavior patterns, and change those patterns as you discover them to be inappropriate. Thus, you have this opportunity to teach yourself, rather than to criticize others.

You should keep notes about key events during the simulation. Use the between-session breaks to make notes for yourself to facilitate later recall of key events and important learning experiences.

GLOBAL ORGANIZATION

OrgSim® is three hours of an integrated experimental design with a proposed panel of experts in the field of international development and business.

The 80 minutes would revolve around a new version of The Organization Simulation called "OrgSim® Global." In this simulated global corporation a designated headquarters staff must work with corporate manufacturing units operating in four regions of the world: Asia, Europe, Africa/Middle East, and North and South America. In this simulation, global corporate decisions will follow from an imposed scenario of opportunities and constraints given to the participants. The design will be adaptable for a range of 50 to 300 participants.

As the simulation evolves, the panel of experts will be carefully observing the emergent dynamics in order to prepare their remarks for the last half of the session. In addition, feedback will be solicited from the simulation participants in order to surface critical issues about the nature of global business and how best they feel human resource development people can prepare themselves for this coming global scenario.

The session will then provide not only an experimental activity in order to experience firsthand global organizational issues, but also to share with a panel of experts (to include Ken Murrell of West Florida University, Peter Quennell of the United Nations, R. S. Moorthy and/or Pat Canavan of Motorola, and BJ Chakiris) the concerns and issues that emerge from facing directly the cross-cultural and business dynamics of a global environment.

The OrgSim is being used by a number of organizations, including Motorola University Management Institute II, Ace Corporation, Kodak, and graduate schools of policy and administration.

Appendix E

The Four Myths of International Management

Taken from "Preparing Managers for Foreign Assignments"
–Edward Dunbar and Allan Katcher
Training & Development Journal
September 1990

It is 10:20 A.M. and John is sitting at his desk, rereading the job description of district sales manager in Caracas—his new position. It's a promotion for John, but he's nervous about such a big move. He's never been to South America and isn't sure what to expect. When John mentioned his concern to his boss, she just clapped him on the back, said, "Don't worry; you'll be terrific!" and changed the subject.

Two floors away, Susan, the director of international personnel, is reviewing the file of a manager returning from four years in Hong Kong. He has been solely responsible for the company's southeast Asian operations, and Susan is at a loss as to where to place him back in the United States. No comparable position exists; even a promotion would involve less responsibility.

With the international scope of most large organizations today and the continuing move to offshore manufacturing in the third world, scenarios such as these are not unusual. Firms frequently feel compelled to expatriate staff, but most companies do not have a clearly defined human resources program to support international managers.

In a recent study conducted at Columbia University with *Fortune* 500 international personnel managers, 70 percent of the respondents reported that expatriates were sent abroad when local candidates were not available. In a third of the cases, high-potential domestic employees were the preferred candidates to relocate abroad. But only 30 percent to 45 percent of the multinational corporations in the study provided some form of cross-cultural orientation to expatriates.

In our work with international personnel managers, we've identified four types of international managers, depending on their ability to adjust to conditions abroad.

1. **Our person in Havana** describes the well-connected company employee, who experiences little difficulty in adjusting or performing in a foreign country. Companies that view the foreign assignment this way do relatively little for their staff. Personnel managers who rely too much upon this myth will think of life in a large city such as Los Angeles, California, as the same as that in Jakarta, Indonesia, emphasizing the similarities to the exclusion of the differences.

2. **The lost employee** myth holds that the person who is out of sight is out of mind. Such employees are isolated from the domestic realities of the firm and are uncertain as to when or if they are to repatriate—or if there will be a position for them on their return.

For such employees, expatriation is bad in terms of organizational politics. In an organization that views expatriation this way, repatriated managers usually have limited input to the home office regarding policy or business strategy abroad. One U.S. personnel manager said he never wanted to see his expatriate managers return for home leave during their assignments, and that he did not want to repatriate them within the company after their return.

3. **The ugly American** myth describes the expatriate who is unfamiliar with the cultural realities of the host country. "Ugly Americans" are not just unhappy living abroad; they are a liability to their firms. (Although in some cases, the truly culture-blind international employee may actually experience less stress than one who is actively engaged with the host culture.) The less people are aware of their own cultural biases, the less competent they will be in work relationships with foreign nationals.

4. **Cultural relativists** find relocation challenging both personally and professionally. These people are good at working with others and enjoy it, so the company assumes they will adapt easily. As with the our-person-in-Havana myth, companies that believe their employees are cultural relativists are likely to ignore adjustment problems and missed business opportunities.

The reality of the expatriate's situation, of course, lies somewhere between the stereotypes. Some managers will succeed under any circumstances, others would clearly benefit from a comprehensive human resources program, and others—even those who have been solid performers in the United States—will be liabilities abroad, even under the best of circumstances. Subscribing to any of the myths prevents a company from truly preparing its international managers for success.

Merck Manufacturing Division—CD-I Pharmaceutical Manufacturing Worldwide Training

COMPACT DISC INTERACTIVE OVERVIEW

What is CD-I?

Compact Disc Interactive (CD-I) is a high-performance, self-contained interactive multimedia information delivery system based on a global standard.

CD-I addresses applications in the industrial marketplace for training, education, sales, and marketing, as well as the consumer marketplace for entertainment, information, and education.

CD-I is cost-effective and easy to use, and is based on a standardized architecture agreed to and supported by more than 100 manufacturers and producers worldwide.

This evolutionary technology combines text, graphics, animation, video, still images, and audio onto a 5¼-inch disc for use in a CD-I player.

Features of CD-I

- Plays any CD-I discs, regardless of make, manufacturer, or country of origin.
- Plays all audio CD discs, Kodak's Photo CD discs, and CD Rom XA "bridge" discs.
- Uses digital video and audio processing.

- Uses a multimedia controller (MMC) that controls, plays, and runs the interactive program.
- Can store more than 7,000 photographic images.
- Allows for 72 minutes of full-screen, full-motion animation.
- Has image capabilities for more than 16-million color variations.
- Engineered with four levels of sound qualities: CD-DA, Hi-Fi, Mid-Fi, and Speech.
- Has four video screens: cursor, background, and two intermediate.

WHY USE CD-I FOR INTERNATIONAL TRAINING?

Simple to Use

In developing an interactive multimedia training program, you must consider how complex your hardware system will be. The CD-I system consists of a CD-I player (about the size of the first CD audio players), a pointer device or mouse, and a television set or monitor. No other equipment is required.

Worldwide Standards

CD-I, like CD digital audio (CD-DA), is a worldwide standard. Any disc will work in any player throughout the world. There are more than 100 companies worldwide licensed to make CD-I players.

Multilingual Capability

This is one of the most compelling reasons to use CD-I for international training programs. Because of CD-I's high-storage capacity (650 megabytes and up to eight stereo audio tracks), one disc can hold enough data to present the same material in several languages simultaneously. This allows the same disc to be used worldwide.

Interactive

By combining audio, video, text, graphics, still pictures, and animation you can create a personal dialogue between user and machine. This experience is a blend of enjoyment and benefit. Studies demonstrate that interactive capability can result in a 40 percent greater retention value from the presented information materials than from any other source.

Addresses NTSC and PAL

Throughout the world there are two basic standards for television sets: NTSC is used in the United States and Japan and PAL is used in Europe and South America. When developing international programs, PAL should be used, allowing the user to view titles on both NTSC and PAL television sets.

Power Supply Selections

The Philips Professional 602 player has the ability to address both 110 and 220 volt systems and adjusts automatically to 50/60 cycle.

Low-Cost Hardware Platform

The cost of a CD-I system is currently about a third of the cost of a personal computer-based multimedia configuration that requires CD ROM drives, video boards, and different keyboards for international use.

Cost of CD-I Discs

The cost of mastering and replicating CD-I discs is significantly less than other similar types of storage transfer media.

Reliable

The Philips Industrial Player has a mean time between failures (MTBF) of 35,000 hours, so hardware failures should be exceedingly rare.

Easy to Service

If an interactive videodisc, or other computer-based system experiences a hardware failure, the result is usually an expensive and time-consuming site visit by a trained maintenance technician. This can be very costly, especially on an international basis. CD-I is a self-contained unit. A replacement can be shipped overnight and installed in a matter of minutes.

Ongoing Cost

Because CD-I is a low-cost interactive system, service maintenance contracts are far less costly than more expensive computer-based systems.

HARDWARE—CD-I VERSUS PC-BASED SYSTEMS

CD-I Design

CD-I was designed from the ground up as a self-contained interactive multimedia system. It uses a real-time operating system that can process text, video, audio, and animation at a high rate of speed without adding hardware components.

PC Design

To function as real-time interactive multimedia systems, PC-based systems need additional and expensive internal boards for processing sound and digital video. These systems must also be configured with internal or external CD-ROM drives.

CD-I Standards

Worldwide standards. Any disc will play on any player anywhere in the world.

PC Standards

These systems can be Industry Standard Architecture, Micro Channel based, or Apple based. There are also additional MPC standards established for multimedia-based PC systems.

CD-I International Setup

The professional player uses a universal power supply for 110/220 and 50/60 cycle current. The unit is a self-contained plug-and-play unit. No additional hardware is required other than a monitor or television. CD-I also handles PAL television standards used in Europe and South America, and NTSC which is used in the United States and Japan.

PC International Setup

These units may or may not have universal power supplies. Based on the configuration of the system. CD ROM drives can be internal or external— all systems must be configurated with an operating system and the appropriate keyboard designed for each country.

CD-I Dependability

35,000-hour MTBF, which is equivalent to nearly four years of operating 24 hours per day, 365 days per year. Or at 40 hours per week—almost 17 years of operation.

PC Dependability

Only as dependable as the weakest link in a multiple-piece configuration.

CD-I Costs

The total cost of a CD-I player is $1,600. If you add a monitor with built-in speakers your total price is $2,100.

PC Costs

PC-based systems require a high-end system 386 processor or better in order to perform at a similar level to CD-I. By adding video, audio, and digital video interactive (DVI) boards; speakers; CD ROM II drive; and a high-end monitor, the total cost of a multimedia interactive system can cost as much as $7,500.

Costs Comparison

The following chart shows a comparison in hardware cost for multiple installations. The cost for both a CD-I and PC-based system is based on the following:

CD-I system
- CD-I 602 professional player $1,595.00
                                            $1,595.00

IBM PC-Based System

- IBM PS/2 Ultimedia model M57 SLC $4,840.00
- IBM model 8515 14-inch monitor   915.00
- IBM ActionMedia II (DVI board)   1,695.00
- Operating system   100.00

                       $7,550.00

NOTE: CD-I uses a television set. A computer monitor is required for PC based systems.

System cost comparison chart			
# of Units	CD-I Cost ($1,595)	PC Cost ($7,550)	CD-I Hardware Savings
25	$ 39,875	$ 188,750	$ 148,875
50	79,750	377,500	297,750
100	159,500	755,000	595,500
150	239,250	1,132,500	893,250
200	319,000	1,510,000	1,191,000
250	398,750	1,887,500	1,488,750

OVERVIEW OF CD-I VERSUS DVI

Overview

Many people think that DVI and CD-I are similar products, they are not.

DVI Technology

DVI is a compression methodology supported by IBM and Intel for showing full-motion video on a computer screen. This technology requires a special board that must be added to the base computer system. IBM is currently offering the ActionMedia II board, which is priced at $1,695. This board is required if you want to run DVI on a computer-based system.

CD-I Technology

CD-I is an interactive multimedia platform. It is a self-contained player that is connected to a televison set or monitor. No computer system is needed to run CD-I full-motion video.

Comparison

DVI	versus	CD-I
High hardware cost		Low hardware cost
No international standard		International standard
Multiple configuration required		Self-contained unit
Requires storage of information on floppy, hard disc, and CD ROM		Entire software program on a CD disc

Conclusion

When you consider the high cost of DVI, along with the costs of servicing computer-based systems, CD-I with its self-contained, easy-to-maintain, and international standards appears ideally suited for Merck's purposes.

Notes

Introduction

1. "Distinguishing a Car's Nationality Requires a Global Perspective," *The Dallas Morning News*, Dallas, TX, February 22, 1992.

2. Neal Rubin, "'Buy American' Would Play Havoc with Toy Prices," *The Dallas Morning News*, Dallas, TX, February 18, 1992.

3. Marcia Kirkpatrick, "Why Aren't American Firms Training for Global Participation?" *Management Development Report*, ASTD, Alexandria, VA, Summer 1990.

4. Ibid.

5. Ibid.

6. Clifford Clarke, president of Clarke Consulting, ASTD Task Force Meeting in San Francisco, CA, May 1991.

7. Serge Ogranovich, partner, Center for intercultural training and education, ASTD Task Force Meeting in San Francisco, CA, May 1991.

8. Nessa Lowenthal, president of Transitions Unlimited, ASTD Task Force Meeting in San Francisco, CA, May 1991.

9. Gary M. Wederspahn, "Cross-Cultural Services: Guidelines for Consumers," *Mobility*, January/February 1986.

10. Ibid.

11. Ibid.

12. International Orientation Resource's Survey, "The Selection of Candidates for Overseas Assignments," July 1, 1991.

13. Vince A. Miller, *The Guidebook for International Trainers in Business and Industry*, New York: Van Nostrand Reinhold and ASTD, 1979.

14. Interview with Ralph Dosher, Stan Horner, and Roy Pendergrass, former employees of Texas Instruments, Dallas, TX, 1992.

15. Presentation by Don Botto, director of corporate quality planning, The Goodyear Tire Company, ASTD pre-conference workshop, New Orleans, LA, May 1992.

16. Interview with Bill Jones, international personnel manager, General Dynamics Corporation, Fort Worth, TX, 1992.

17. Interview with Geraldine M. Thornsberry, manager of international operations, AT&T, Morristown, NJ, 1992.

18. Interview with Eldon Arden, manager of management development, 3M, St. Paul, MN, 1992.

19. Interview with Cindy Johnson, manager of supervisory and individual development programs, 3M, St. Paul, MN, 1992.

20. Interview with Dave Dresden, director of international assignments, Baxter International, Deerfield, IL, 1992.

Chapter 1

1. Patricia A. Galagan, "Executive Development in a Changing World," *Training & Development Journal*, June 1990.

2. Nancy Adler and Fariborz Ghadar, "Human Resource Management: A Global Perspective," *Human Resource Management in International Comparison*, Rudiger Pieper (ed.), Berlin/New York: Walter de Gruyter, 1990.

3. Ibid.

4. Stephen H. Rhinesmith, *A Manager's Guide to Globalization*, Homewood, IL: ASTD and Business One Irwin, 1992.

5. Ibid.

6. Adler and Ghadar, "Human Resource Management: A Global Perspective."

7. Gary M. Wederspahn, "Cross-Cultural Services: Guidelines for Consumers," *Mobility*, January/February 1986.

8. Marcia Kirkpatrick, "Why Aren't American Firms Training for Global Participation?" *Management Development Report*, ASTD, Summer 1990.

9. Data collection aspects from Chris Fowler, Creative Human Resource Consultants.

10. A. Lee Schomer, former international training manager, Caltex Corporation, assisted with the sample survey development.

11. Lorraine Parker, "Collecting Data the E-Mail Way," *Training & Development*, July 1992.

Chapter 2

1. Nancy Adler and Susan Bartholomew, "Managing Globally Competent People," *Academy of Management Executive*, August 1992.

2. Gareth Morgan, *Riding the Waves of Change: Developing Managerial Competencies for a Turbulent World*, San Francisco, CA: Jossey-Bass, 1988.

3. Peter B. Vaill, *Managing as a Performing Art: New Ideas for a World of Chaotic Change*, San Francisco, CA: Jossey-Bass, 1989.

4. Stephen H. Rhinesmith, *A Manager's Guide To Globalization*, Homewood, IL: ASTD and Business One Irwin, 1992.

5. Patricia A. Galagan, "Executive Development in a Changing World," *Training & Development Journal*, June 1990.

6. Lawrence W. Tuller, *Going Global*, Homewood, IL: Business One Irwin, 1991.

Chapter 3

1. George S. Yip, *Total Global Strategy*, New York: Prentice-Hall, Inc., 1992.

2. Stephen H. Rhinesmith, "An Agenda for Globalization," *Training & Development Journal*, February 1991.

3. Bob Filipczak, "The Business of Training at NCR," *Training*, February 1992.

4. Ralph Catalanello and John Redding, "Three Strategic Training Roles," *Training & Development Journal*, December 1989.

5. Jerry W. Gilley, *Strategic Planning for Human Resource Development*, ASTD Info-Line, June 1992.

6. William Wiggenhorn, "Motorola U: When Training Becomes an Education," *Harvard Business Review*, July-August 1990.

7. Interview with Gordon Bennett, global training manager, ABB Process Automation, Rochester, NY, September, 1992.

8. Stephen H. Rhinesmith, *A Manager's Guide To Globalization*, Homewood, IL: Business One Irwin, 1992.

9. Ellen Brandt, "Global HR," *Personnel Journal*, March 1992.

Chapter 4

1. J. F. Wedman and M. Tessmer, "The Layers of Necessity ID Model," *Performance and Instruction*, 29, no. 41, April 1990.

2. *AFS Orientation Handbook*, Vol. IV, 1984.

3. Ibid.

4. D. A. Ralston; D. J. Gustafson; P. M. Elsass; and R. H. Terpstra, "Eastern Values: A Comparison of Managers in the United States, Hong Kong, and the People's Republic of China, *Journal of Applied Psychology*, 77, no. 5, 1992.

5. P. R. Harris and R. T. Moran, *Managing Cultural Differences*, Houston, TX: Gulf Publishing, 1991.

6. Geert Hofstede, *Cultures and Organizations: Software of the Mind*, New York: McGraw-Hill, 1991.

7. E. Tulving, "How Many Memory Systems Are There?" *American Psychologist*, 40, 1985.

8. G.L. Nelson, "The Implications of Schema Theory Reading Research to Technology Transfer in Developing Countries," in *Proceedings of the Human Factors Society—34th Annual Meeting*, 1990.

9. R. M. Gagne and R. Glaser, "Foundations in Learning Research," in *Instructional Techniques: Foundations*, Hillsdale, NJ: Erlbaum, 1987.

10. C. Bereiter and M. Scardamalia, "Cognitive Coping Strategies and the Problem of 'Inert' Knowledge," in *Thinking and Learning Skills: Current Research and Open Questions*, Hillsdale, NJ: Erlbaum, 1985.

11. A. L. Brown; J. C. Campione; and J. D. Day, "Learning To Learn: On Training Students to Learn from Texts," *Educational Researcher*, 10, 1981; J. D. Bransford; R. Sherwood; N. Vye; and J. Reiser, "Teaching Thinking and Problem Solving," *American Psychologist*, 41, 1986.

12. M. Silberman, *Active Training*, New York: Lexington Books, 1990.

13. Barbara Martin, "Internalizing Instructional Design," *Educational Technology*, 24 May, 1984.

14. Glenn E. Snelbecker, "Practical Ways for Using Theories and Innovations to Improve Training," in George Piskurich, ed., *The ASTD Handbook of Instructional Technology*, New York: ASTD and McGraw-Hill, 1992.

15. Martin, "Internalizing Instructional Design."

16. Peter Beckschi and David Case of the World Environment Center provided the research and ideas for Chapter 4.

Chapter 5

1. Beverly Geber, "The Care and Breeding of Global Managers," *Training*, July 1992.

2. Ibid.

3. Kenichi Ohmae, *The Borderless World*, New York: Harper Business Press, 1990.

4. Marsha Kirkpatrick, "Why Aren't American Firms Training for Global Participation?" *Management Development Report*, ASTD, Summer 1990.

5. Hal B. Gregersen and J. Stewart Black, "When Yankee Comes Home: Factors Related to Expatriate and Spouse Repatriation Adjustment," *Journal of International Business Studies*, 1991.

6. Kirkpatrick.

7. Moran, Stahl & Boyer International, Boulder, CO.

8. International Training Associates of Princeton, Princeton, NJ.

9. Training Management Corporation, Princeton, NJ.

10. Trans Cultural Services, Portland, OR.

11. DeVaney-Wong International, Warrenton, VA.

12. INSERV, Dallas, TX.

13. Lawton International, Oklahoma City, OK.

14. Moran, Stahl & Boyer International, Boulder, CO.

15. Intercultural Development, Inc., Solana Beach, CA.

16. International Orientation Resources, Northbrook, IL.

17. Global Interact, Dallas, TX.

18. Priscila C. Montana & Associates, Dallas, TX.

19. Pachter and Associates, Cherry Hill, NJ.

20. Intercultural Development, Inc., Solana Beach, CA.

21. INSERV, Dallas, TX.

22. Bennett Associates, Chicago, IL.

23. Global Dynamics, Inc., Randolph, NJ.

24. Peter Senge, *The Fifth Discipline—The Art and Practice of the Learning Organization*, New York: Doubleday, 1990.

25. Training Management Corporation, Princeton, NJ.

26. International Orientation Resources, Northbrook, IL.

27. Global Dynamics, Inc., Randolph, NJ.

28. Center for intercultural training and education, Vienna, VA.

29. Intercultural Development, Inc., Solana Beach, CA.

30. Sally Normand McReynolds, San Francisco, CA.

31. Global Interact, Dallas, TX.

32. Global Dynamics, Inc., Randolph, NJ.

33. Moran, Stahl & Boyer International, Boulder, CO.

34. Intercultural Development, Inc., Solana Beach, CA.

35. International Training Association of Princeton, Princeton, NJ.

36. Global Dynamics, Inc., Randolph, NJ.

37. INSERV, Dallas, TX.

38. Global Dynamics, Inc., Randolph, NJ.

39. George Renwick, Renwick and Associates, Carefree, AZ.

40. Moran, Stahl & Boyer International, Boulder, CO.

41. International Training Associates of Princeton, Princeton, NJ.

42. Clarke Consulting Group, Inc., Redwood City, CA.

43. Global Dynamics, Inc., Randolph, NJ.

44. International Training Associates fo Princeton, Princeton, NJ.

45. Training Management Corporation, Princeton, NJ.

46. Bennett Associates, Chicago, IL.

47. Moran, Stahl & Boyer International, Boulder, CO.

48. Clarke Consulting Group, Inc. Redwood City, CA.

49. East-West Consultants, Lafayette, CA.

50. Beverly Geber, "The Care and Breeding of Global Managers," *Training*, July 1992.

51. International Orientation Resources, Northbrook, IL.

52. The WORLD Group, Betheseda, MD.

53. Training Management Corporation, Princeton, NJ.

54. International Training Associates of Princeton, Princeton, NJ.

55. Training Management Corporation, Princeton, NJ.

56. Moran, Stahl & Boyer International, Boulder, CO.

57. International Orientation Resources, Northbrook, IL.

58. LinguaCall International, Inc., Glenside, CA.

59. Charles M. Vance, "Preparing the Host Country Workforce for Expatriate Managers: The Neglected Other Side of the Coin," International Conference of the Eastern Academy of Management, Nice, France, June 1991, and "An Ethical Argument for Host Country Workforce Training as Part of the Expatriate Management Assignment," (with Eduardo S. Paderon and John T. Wholihan), the 3rd Conference on International Personnel and Human Resources Management, Ashridge Management College, Hertfordshire, U.K., July 1992.

60. Charles M. Vance, "A Refocus Upon the Role of the Mexican Workforce in Improving Expatriate Manager Success with the *Maquiladora* Assignment," the 4th Annual International Conference of the Society for the Advancement of Socio-Economics, UC-Irvine, California, March 1992, and "A Comparative Analysis of Host Country National Training Design Needs in Five Countries of the Pacific Rim" (with David M. Boje and H. Daniel Stage), Annual Meeting of the Western Academy of Management, Santa Barbara, California, March 1991.

61. J. Stewart Black and Mark Mendenhall, "A Practical but Theory-Based Framework for Selecting Cross-Cultural Training Methods," *Human Resource Management*, Winter 1989.

62. Mark Mendenhall and Gary Oddou, "Acculturation Profiles of Expatriate Managers: Implications for Cross-Cultural Training Programs," *Columbia Journal of World Business*, vol. 21, 1986.

63. Black and Mendenhall, "A Practical but Theory-Based Framework for Selecting Cross-Cultural Training Methods."

64. Interview with Sharon Richards, intercultural training manager, Intel, Portola Valley, CA, 1992.

65. Interview with Mary Anne Williams, corporate director of executive education, Eastman Kodak, Rochester, NY, 1992.

66. Interview with Michael Copeland, international training and development manager, Procter & Gamble, Cincinnati, OH, 1992.

67. BJ Chakiris Corporation, Chicago, IL.

68. Black and Mendenhall, "A Practical but Theory-Based Framework for Selecting Cross-Cultural Training Methods."

Chapter 6

1. Madelyn R. Callahan, "Preparing the New Global Manager," *Training & Development Journal*, March 1989.

2. International Orientation Resources, "The Selection of Candidates for Overseas Assignment," July 1, 1991.

3. Moran, Stahl & Boyer International, Boulder, CO.

4. Presentation by Barry Kozloff, Selection Research International, Inc., ASTD preconference workshop, New Orleans, LA, May 1992.

5. Roger L. M. Dunbar and Allan Bird, professors at Stern School of Business, New York University, cited in "Calling on Electronics to Limit Culture Shock," *The Wall Street Journal*, May, 4, 1992 and "Creative Experiential Techniques for Management Development," *The Journal of Management Development*, vol. II, no. 7 (1992).

6. Interchange International.

7. Interview with Evelyn Mareth, Interchange U.S.A., Fairfield, CT, October 1992.

8. Noel Kreicker, president of International Orientation Resources, July 1992, "Dual-Career Couples: The Impact of the International Assignment."

9. Presentation by William D. Shea, director of the Center for Creative Leadership's European office in Brussels, Belgium, ASTD pre-conference workshop, New Orleans, LA, May 1992.

10. Margaret Cohn, "What It Takes to be a Global Manager in the 1990s," *Innovations in International Compensation*, August 1990.

11. Selma Myers, consultant, "Basics of Intercultural Communication," ASTD Info-Line, Alexandria, VA, September 1990.

12. Cohn, "What It Takes to be a Global Manager in the 1990s."

13. Presentation by Arash Afshar, International Consultants for Management and Development, and Adrienne Anderson, The Global Consortium, ASTD pre-conference workshop, New Orleans, LA, May 1992.

14. Interview with Jean Michel Boisvert, training analyst for the Department of National Revenue in Québec, Canada, October 1992.

15. Beverly Geber, "The Care and Breeding of Global Managers," *Training*, July 1992.

16. Ibid.

17. Ibid.

18. Interview with Irene Denigris, international recruitment and development program administration, Johnson & Johnson, Colts Neck, NJ, October 1992.

19. Geert Hofstede, "Culture in the Workplace."

20. Geber, "The Care and Breeding of Global Managers."

21. "UPS Works to Absorb Its European Acquisitions," *Business International*, August 24, 1992.

22. Ibid.

23. J. Stewart Black, Hal B. Gregersen, and Mark Mendenhall, *Global Assignments — Successfully Expatriating and Repatriating International Managers*, San Francisco, CA: Jossey-Bass, 1992.

24. Presentation by Joyce Rogers, international training specialist, MCI, ASTD preconference workshop, New Orleans, LA, May 1992.

25. Gary M. Wederspahn, "Working With Interpreters," *Cultural Diversity at Work*, November 1991.

26. Michael Paige, ed., "Trainer Competencies for International and Intercultural Programs," in *Education for the Intercultural Experience*, Yarmouth, ME, Intercultural Press, 1993.

27. Interview with Gordon Bennett, global training manager for ASEA Brown Boveri Process Automation, Rochester, NY, September 1992.

28. Ibid.

Chapter 7

1. James L. Noel and Ram Charan, "GE Brings Global Thinking to Light," *Training & Development*, June 1992.

2. Nancy Adler and Susan Bartholomew, "Managing Globally Competent People," *Academy of Management Executive*, August 1992.

3. Carla Rapoport, "A Tough Swede Invades the U.S.," *Fortune*, June 29, 1992.

4. Margaret Cohn, "What It Takes to Be a Global Manager in the 1990s," *Innovations in International Compensation*, August 1990.

5. Adler and Bartholomew, "Managing Globally Competent People."

6. Interview with Steve Merman, training director, Amoco Production Company, Chicago, IL, 1991.

7. Presentation by K. L. Cheah, director of planning, Motorola University, ASTD pre-conference workshop, New Orleans, LA, May 1992.

8. Presentation by Albert Scius, European director of training, Coulter Corporation, Hialeah, FL, ASTD pre-conference workshop, New Orleans, LA, May 1992.

9. Presentation by Steve Ginsburgh, manager of organizational services and employee development, Maxus Energy Corporation, Dallas, TX, ASTD pre-conference workshop, New Orleans, LA, May 1992.

10. Lawrence Tuller, *Going Global*, Homewood, IL: Business One Irwin, 1991.

11. Presentation by William D. Shea, director of the Center for Creative Leadership's European office in Brussels, Belgium, ASTD pre-conference workshop, New Orleans, LA, May 1992.

12. Gary M. Wederspahn, "Cross-Cultural Services: Guidelines for Consumers," *Mobility*, January/February 1986.

13. Michael J. Copeland, "International Training," in *Training and Development Handbook: A Guide to Human Resource Development*, 3d Ed., Robert L. Craig, editor-in-chief, New York: McGraw-Hill, 1987.

14. Christopher A. Bartlett and Sumantra Ghosal, "What Is a Global Manager?" *Harvard Business Review*, September-October 1992.

Bibliography

Adler, Nancy. *International Dimensions of Organizational Behavior*. Boston, MA: Kent Publishing, 1986.

Adler, Nancy, and Susan Bartholomew. "Managing Globally Competent People." *Academy of Management Executive*, August 1992.

Adler, Nancy, and Fariborz Ghadar. "Human Resource Management: A Global Perspective." *Human Resource Management in International Comparison*. Rudiger Pieper, ed., Berlin, Germany: Walter de Gruyter, 1990.

Adler, Nancy, and Dafina N. Izraeli, eds. *Women in Management Worldwide*. Armonk, NY: M.E. Sharpe, 1988.

Adler, Nancy and R. B. Peterson. "Expatriate Selection and Failure." *Human Resource Planning*, vol. 14, 1991.

AFS Orientation Handbook, Vol. IV. American Field Service, 1984.

Akande, Adebowale. "A Programme for Training Trainers in Nigeria." *Industrial & Commercial Training*, 1991.

Ali-Ali, Salahaldeen. "The Role of Training and Education in Technology Transfer: A Case Study of Kuwait." *Technovation*, 1988.

Andrews, D. H., and L. A. Goodson. "A Comparative Analysis of Models of Instructional Design." *Journal of Instructional Development*, Vol. 3, 1980.

Anthony, Peg, and Lincoln A. Norton. "Link HR to Corporate Strategy." *Personnel Journal*, April 1991.

Arkin, Anat. "Insuring Against Insularity." *Personnel Management*, June 1991.

Armstrong, Richard N. "Cross-Cultural Communication Training in Business: A Sensitizing Model." Ypsilanti, MI: Eastern Michigan University Report, 1988.

Arvidson, Lars, and Kjell Rubenson. "Education and Training of the Labor Force in the EFTA Countries." Report prepared for the seminar "New Challenges in the Education and Training of the European Workforce" (Stockholm, Sweden, June 13–14, 1990). National Swedish Board Education, Stockholm, 1991.

Atiyyah, Hamid S. "Effectiveness of Management Training in Arab Countries." *Journal of Management Development*, 1991.

Austin, Clyde, ed. *Cross-Cultural Re-Entry*. Abilene, TX: Abilene Christian University Press, 1986.

Barnum, Cynthia, and David R. Gaster. "Global Leadership." *Executive Excellence*, June 1991.

Bartlett, Christopher A., and Sumantra Ghoshal. *Cross-Border Management*. Homewood, IL: Business One Irwin, 1992.

_____. "What Is a Global Manager?" *Harvard Business Review*, September-October 1992.

_____. *Managing Across Borders: The Transnational Solution*. New York: Harvard Business School Press, 1989.

Battaglia, Beverly A. "Skills for Managing Multicultural Teams." *Cultural Diversity at Work*, January 1992.

Beamish, Paul W. et al. *International Management: Text and Cases*. Homewood, IL: Richard D. Irwin, 1991.

Befus, C. P. "A Multilevel Treatment Approach for Culture Shock Experienced By Sojourners." *International Journal of Intercultural Relations*, vol. 12, 1988.

Bennis, Warren. "Leadership in the 21st Century." *Training*, May 1990.

Ben-Yoseph, Miriam. "Designing and Delivering Cross-Cultural Instruction," Ypsilanti, MI: Eastern Michigan University Report, 1988.

Bereiter, C., and M. Scardamalia. "Cognitive Coping Strategies and the Problem of 'Inert' Knowledge." *Thinking and Learning Skills: Current Research and Open Questions*. Hillsdale, NJ: Erlbaum, 1985.

Berger, Michael. "Building Bridges Over Cultural Rivers." *International Management* (UK). vol. 42, no. 7/8, July/August 1987.

Berry, John K. "Linking Management Development to Business Strategies." *Training & Development Journal*, August 1990.

Black, J. Stewart; Hal B. Gregersen; and Mark Mendenhall. *Global Assignments — Successfully Expatriating and Repatriating International Managers*. San Francisco, CA: Jossey-Bass, 1992.

Black, J. Stewart, and Mark Mendenhall. "Cross-Cultural Training Effectiveness: A Review and a Theoretical Framework for Future Research." *Academy of Management Review*, vol. 15, 1990.

_____. "A Practical but Theory-based Framework for Selecting Cross-Cultural Training Methods." *Human Resource Management*, Winter 1989.

Black, J. Stewart; Mark Mendenhall; and Gary R. Oddou. "Towards a Comprehensive Model of International Adjustment: An Integration of Multiple Theoretical Perspectives." *Academy of Management Review*, vol. 16, 1991.

Black, J. Stewart, and G. K. Stephens. "The Influence of the Spouse on American Expatriate Adjustment and Intent to Stay in Pacific Rim Assignments." *Journal of Management*, vol. 15, 1989.

Blocklyn, Paul L. "Developing the International Executive." *Personnel*, March 1989.

Borisoff, Deborah, and David A. Victor. *Conflict Management: A Communication Skills Approach*. New York: Prentice-Hall, 1989.

Brandt, Ellen. "Global HR." *Personnel Journal*, March 1992.

Bransford, J. D.; R. Sherwood; N. Vye; and J. Reiser. "Teaching Thinking and Problem Solving." *American Psychologist*, 41, 1986.

Brislin, R. W. *Cross-Cultural Encounters*. Oxford, England: Pergamon Press, 1981.

"Britain: Getting Into Training." *Economist*, January 25, 1992.

Brislin, R. W. et al. *Intercultural Interactions: A Practical Guide*. Newbury Park, CA: Sage Publications, 1985.

Brown, A. L.; J. C. Campione; and J. D. Day. "Learning To Learn: On Training Students to Learn from Texts." *Educational Researcher*, 10, 1981.

Callahan, Madelyn R. "Preparing the New Global Manager," *Training & Development*, March 1989.

Campbell, Clifton P., and Gerald D. Cheek. "Vocational Training in Switzerland." *Journal Industrial Teacher Education*, Fall 1991.

Carnevale, Anthony Patrick. *America and the New Economy: How New Competitive Standards are Radically Changing the American Workplace*. San Francisco, CA: Jossey-Bass, 1991.

Caropreso, Frank, ed. "Managing Globally: Key Perspectives." Conference Board, Report No. 972, 1991.

Carr, Clay. "The Three R's of Training." *Training*, June 1992.

Casmir, F. L., ed. *International and Intercultural Communication*. Lanham, MD: University Press of America, 1978.

_____. *International and Intercultural Communication Annual*, Volume 3. Speech Communication Association, 1976.

_____. *International and Intercultural Communication Annual*, Volume 2. Speech Communication Association, 1975.

_____. *International and Intercultural Communication Annual*, Volume 1. Speech Communication Association, 1974.

Casner-Lotto, Jill. "Successful Training Strategies: Twenty-six Innovative Corporate Models." *Training Process/HRD Strategic Planning*, San Francisco, CA: Jossey-Bass, 1988.

Casse, Pierre. *Training for the Multicultural Manager*. Washington, D.C.: Society of Intercultural Education Training Research (SIETAR), 1982.

_____. *Training for the Cross-Cultural Mind*. 2d ed. Washington, D.C.: Society of Intercultural Education Training Research (SIETAR), 1981.

Catalanello, Ralph, and John Redding. "Three Strategic Training Roles." *Training & Development Journal*, December 1989.

Caudron, Shari. "Training Ensures Success Overseas." *Personnel Journal*, December 1991.

_____. "Training Helps United Go Global." *Personnel Journal*, February 1992.

Chowanec, Gregory D., and Charles N. Newstrom. "The Strategic Management of International Human Resources." *Business Quarterly* (University of Western Ontario), Autumn 1991.

Cocheu, Ted. "Integrating Training with Quality Strategy." *Technical & Skills Training*, February/March 1992.

Cohn, Margaret. "What It Takes to be a Global Manager in the 1990s." *Innovations in International Compensation*, August 1990.

Condon, J.C. *Good Neighbors, Communicating with Mexicans*. Yarmouth, ME: Intercultural Press, Inc., 1985.

Conference Board. *Building Global Teamwork for Growth and Survival*. The Conference Board, Research Bulletin No. 228, 1990.

Cooney, Barry D. "Japan and America: Culture Counts." *Training & Development Journal*. vol. 43, no. 8, August 1989.

Cooper, John. "Tailoring Education and Training to Labour Market Requirements." *International Journal of Manpower*, 1991.

Copeland, Lennie, and Lewis Briggs. *Going International: How to Make Friends and Deal Effectively in the International Marketplace*. New York: Random House, 1985.

Coupland, Lester. "Developing European Trainers." *Industrial & Commercial Training*, 1991.

Craig, R. L., ed. *Training & Development Handbook, A Guide to Human Resource Development* 3d ed. New York: ASTD and McGraw-Hill, 1987.

Crump, Larry. "Japanese Managers–Western Workers: Cross-Cultural Training and Development Issues." *Journal of Management Development* (UK). vol. 8, no. 4, 1989.

deForest, Mariah E. "When in Mexico...." *Business Mexico*, July 1991.

Desatnick, Robert L., and Margo L. Bennett. *Human Resource Management in the Multinational Company*. Westmead, England: Gower Press, 1977.

Doktor, Robert, ed. *International HRD Annual*, volume 1. Alexandria, VA: ASTD, 1985.

Dole, G. E. et al., eds. *Essays in the Science of Culture in Honor of Leslie A. White*. New York: Thomas Y. Crowell Company, 1960.

Domsch, M., and B. Lichtenberger. "Managing the Global Manager: Predeparture Training and Development for German Expatriates in China and Brazil." *Journal of Management Development*, 1991.

Doz, Yves. *Strategic Management in International Companies*. Oxford, England: Pergamon Press, 1986.

Doz, Yves; C. A. Bartlett; and C. K. Prahalad. "Global Competitive Pressures vs. Host Country Demands: Managing the Tensions in Multinational Corporations." *California Management Review*, 23, no. 3, 1981.

Doz, Yves and C. K. Prahalad. *Multinational Companies' Missions: Balancing National Responsiveness and Global Integration*. New York: The Free Press, 1987.

_____. "Controlled Variety: A Challenge for Human Resource Management in the Multinational Corporation. *Human Resource Management,* 25, no. 1, 1986.

Dunbar, E., and M. Ehrlich. *International Human Resource Practices, Selecting, Training, and Managing the International Staff: A Survey Report.* The Project on International Human Resources. New York: Columbia University-Teachers College, 1986.

Early, P. C. "Intercultural Training for Managers: A Comparison of Documentary and Interpersonal Methods." *Academy of Management Journal,* 30.

Evans, Paul. "Strategies for Human Resource Management in Complex Multinational Corporations: A European Perspective." In V. Pucik's Academy of Management Proposal, *Emerging Human Resource Management Strategies in Multinational Firms: A Tricontinental Perspective,* 1987.

_____. "The Strategic Outcomes of Human Resource Management." *Human Resource Management,* 25, 1, 1986.

Evans, Paul; Yves Doz; and Andre Laurent, eds. *Human Resource Management in International Firms: Change, Globalization, Innovation.* New York: St. Martin's Press, 1990.

Felkins, Patricia Kay; BJ Chakiris; and Kenneth N. Chakiris. "Global Consultation." In *Change Consultation.* White Plains, NY: Quality Resources, 1993.

Ferguson, Henry. *Tomorrow's Global Executive.* Homewood, IL: Dow Jones-Irwin, 1988.

Filipczak, Bob. "The Business of Training at NCR." *Training,* February 1992.

Fisher, Glen. *International Negotiation, A Cross-Cultural Perspective.* Yarmouth, ME: Intercultural Press, Inc., 1980.

_____. *Mindsets: The Role of Culture and Perception in International Relations.* Yarmouth, ME: Intercultural Press, 1988.

Fitz-enz, Jac. *Human Value Management.* San Francisco, CA: Jossey-Bass, 1990.

Fitzgerald, Patricia L. "HRD for the Global Age." *Training & Development Journal,* June 1987.

Flynn, Brian H. "The Challenge of Multinational Sales Training." *Training & Development Journal.* vol. 41, no. 11, November 1987.

Foeman, Anita K. "Managing Multiracial Institutions: Goals and Approaches for Race-Relations Training." *Communication Education,* July 1991.

_____. "Race-Relations Training as the Asking of Questions." Paper presented at the 1991 annual meeting of the Eastern Communication Association, April 1991.

Fombrun, Charles; Noel M. Tichy; and Mary Anne Devana. *Strategic Human Resource Management.* New York: John Wiley & Sons, 1984.

Frank, Eric, and Roger Bennett. "HRD in Eastern Europe." *Journal of European Industrial Training,* 1991.

Frankenstein, John, and Hassan Hosseini. "Essential Training for Japanese Duty." *Management Review.* vol. 77, no. 7, July 1988.

Furnham, A., and S. Bochner. *Culture Shock.* New York: Methuen, 1986.

Gagne, R. M., and R. Glaser. "Foundations in Learning Research," in *Instructional Techniques: Foundations.* Hillsdale, NJ: Erlbaum, 1987.

Galagan, Patricia A. "Executive Development in a Changing World." *Training & Development,* June 1990.

Gayeski, Diane M.; Ed Nathan; and Jon Sickle. "Creating a CBT System for Multinational Training." *Interactive Learning International,* January-March 1992.

Geber, Beverly. "The Care and Breeding of Global Managers." *Training,* July 1992.

_____. "A Global Approach to Training." *Training,* vol. 26, no. 9, September 1989.

Ghadar, Fariborz; Philip D. Grub; Robert T. Moran; and Marshall Geer. *Global Business Management in the 1990s.* Washington, D.C.: Beacham Publishing, Inc., 1990.

Gilbert, Nathaniel. "Insulation From Culture Shock: Prepping Employees for Living Overseas." *Trainer's Workshop.* vol. 2, no. 4, October 1987.

Gilley, Jerry W. *Strategic Planning for Human Resource Development.* Alexandria, VA: ASTD Info-Line, June 1992.

Gitter, Robert J. "Job Training in Europe: Lessons From Abroad." *Monthly Labor Review,* April 1992.

Glover, W. G., and G. W. Shames. *World-Class Service.* Yarmouth, ME: Intercultural Press, 1989.

Gregersen, Hal B. "Commitments to a Parent Company and a Local Work Unit During Repatriation." *Personnel Psychology,* Spring 1992.

Gregersen, Hal B., and J. Stewart Black. "When Yankee Comes Home: Factors Related to Expatriate and Spouse Repatriation Adjustment." *Journal of International Business Studies,* vol. 22, 1991.

Griffin, Trenholme J., and W. Russell Daggatt. "The Global Negotiator: Building Strong Business Relationships Anywhere in the World." *Harper Business,* 1990.

Gross, Thomas; Ernie Turner; and Lars Cederholm. "Building Teams for Global Operations." *Management Review,* June 1987.

Grove, Cornelius, and Constance Franklin. "Using the Right Fork Is Just the Beginning: Intercultural Training in the Global Era." *International Public Relations Review,* 13, no. 1, 1990.

Gudykunst, W. B.; M. R. Hammer; and R. L. Wiseman. "An Analysis of an Integrated Approach to Cross-Cultural Training." *International Journal of Intercultural Relations,* no. 1, 1977.

Hales, Larry D. "Training: A Product of Business Planning." *Training & Development Journal,* July 1986.

Hall, Edward T. *Beyond Culture.* New York: Anchor Press/Doubleday, 1976.

_____. *The Hidden Dimension.* New York: Anchor Press, 1969.

Harris, P. R., and R. T. Moran. *Managing Cultural Differences.* 2d ed. Houston, TX: Gulf Publishing Co., 1987.

Hart, P. E., and A. Shipman. "Financing Training in Britain." *National Institute Economic Review*, May 1991.

Hays, R. D. "Expatriate Selection: Insuring Success and Avoiding Failure." *Journal of International Business Studies*, Spring 1974.

Hemphill, David F. "Thinking Hard About Culture in Adult Education: Not a Trivial Pursuit." *Adult Learning*, May 1992.

Hofstede, Geert. *Cultures and Organizations: Software of the Mind*. New York: McGraw-Hill, 1991.

_____. *Culture's Consequences: International Differences in Work Related Values*. Newbury Park, CA: Sage, 1980.

Hoopes, David S., and Paul Ventura, eds. *Intercultural Sourcebook: Cross-Cultural Training Methodologies*. Yarmouth, ME: Intercultural Press, 1979.

Humphrey, Vernon. "Training the Total Organization." *Training & Development* Journal, October 1990.

Ibe, Masanobu, and Noriko Sato. "Educating Japanese Leaders for a Global Age: The Role of the International Education Center." *Journal of Management Development* (UK). vol. 8, no. 4, 1989.

Iyer, S. C. "Problems of Management Development in the Indian Subcontinent." *Journal of Management Development*, 1991.

Jacques, Elliot, and Stephen D. Clement. *Executive Leadership: A Practical Guide to Managing Complexity*. Cambridge, MA: Basil Blackwell, 1991.

Jenkins, Alan. "Training and HR Strategy in France: Discourse and Reality." *Employee Relations*, 1991.

Johnson, Keith R. "Organizational Development in a Context of Opposed Cultural Values: The Case of O.D. in Venezuela." *Organization Development Journal*, Winter 1990.

Johnson, Philip. "Transcending Cultural Differences Through Experiential Teaching Techniques." *Adult Learning*, November 1991.

Johnston, Anton, and Hallgerd Dyrssen. "Cooperation in the Development of Public Sector Management Skills: The SIDA Experience." *Journal of Management Development*, 1991.

Johnston, William B. "Global Workforce 2000: The New World Labor Market." *Harvard Business Review*, March-April 1991.

Jones, Merrick L. "Management Development: An African Focus," *International Studies of Management and Organization*. vol. 19, no. 1, Spring 1989.

Kennedy, Gavin. *Negotiate Anywhere! How to Succeed in International Markets*. London, England: Arrow Books, 1987.

Keys, Bernard, and Robert Wells. "A Global Management Development Laboratory for a Global World." *Journal of Management Development*, 1992.

Kinlaw, Dennis C. *Developing Superior Work Teams*. San Diego, CA: University Associates, 1991.

Kobrin, S. J. "Expatriate Reduction and Strategic Control in American Multinational Corporations." *Human Resource Management*, 27, no. 1, 1986.

Kohls, L. R. *Survival Kit for Overseas Living*, 2nd ed. Yarmouth: ME: Intercultural Press, 1984.

Koopman, Albert. *Transcultural Management: How to Unlock Global Resources*. Cambridge, MA: Basil Blackwell, 1991.

Korn/Ferry International and Columbia School of Business. *21st Century Report: Reinventing the CEO*. New York: Korn/Ferry International, 1989.

Kras, Eva S. *Management in Two Cultures: Bridging the Gap between U.S. and Mexican Managers*. Yarmouth, ME: Intercultural Press, 1989.

Kupfer, Andrew. "How to be a Global Manager." *Fortune*, March 14, 1988.

Lamont, Douglas. *Winning Worldwide: Strategies for Dominating Global Markets*. Homewood, IL: Business One Irwin, 1991.

Landis, D., and R. W. Brislin. *Handbook on Intercultural Training*, volume 1. Oxford, England: Pergamon Press, 1983.

"Language Training." *Personnel Management Plus*, May 1991.

Lanier, A. R. "Selection and Preparation for Overseas Transfers." *Personnel Journal*, 58, 1979.

Latham, G. "Human Resource Training and Development." *Annual Review of Psychology*, 39, 1988.

Laurent, Andre. "The Cross-Cultural Puzzle of Human Resource Management." *Human Resource Management*, 25, no. 1, Spring 1986.

Lazer, Robert I. "Steering Through Turbulence." *Training & Development*, December 1991.

Lobel, Sharon A. "Global Leadership Competencies: Managing to a Different Drumbeat." *Human Resource Management*, 29, no. 1, Spring 1990.

Lorange, P. "Human Resource Management in Multinational Cooperative Ventures." *Human Resource Management*, 25, no. 1, 1986.

Lorenz, Christopher. "The Birth of the 'Transnational'." *The McKinsey Quarterly*, Autumn 1989.

Lubove, Seth. "Ovo Je Line Extension." *Forbes*, July 22, 1991.

Makridakis, Spyros G. et al. *Single Market Europe: Opportunities and Challenges for Business*. San Francisco, CA: Jossey-Bass, 1991.

Manzini, A. O., and J. D. Gridley. *Integrating Human Resources and Strategic Business Planning*. New York: AMACOM, 1986.

Markovitz, David C. "Total Quality Training." *Technical & Skills Training*. Alexandria, VA: ASTD, April 1992.

Marquardt, Michael J., ed. *International HRD*, Volume 3. Alexandria, VA: ASTD, 1987.

Marquardt, Michael J., and Dean W. Engel, *Global Human Resource Development*. New York: Prentice-Hall, 1993.

Marsick, Victoria J., and Lars Cederholm. "Developing Leadership in International Managers—An Urgent Challenge!" *The Columbia Journal of World Business* XXII, no. 4, Winter 1988.

Martin, Barbara "Internalizing Instructional Design." *Educational Technology*, 24, 1984.

McEnery, Jean, and Gaston DesHarnais. "Culture Schock," *Training & Development Journal*, April 1990.

McLearn, Gary N., and Barbara S. Arney. "Advanced Trainers Development Workshop (Islamabad, Pakistan, July 7-26, 1990), Final Report." Academy for Educational Development, August 1990.

Mendenhall, Mark; E. Dunbar; and Gary R. Oddou. "Expatriate Selection, Training, and Career-Pathing: A Review and Critique." *Human Resource Management*, 26, 1978.

Mendenhall, Mark E., and Gary R. Oddou. "Acculturation Profiles of Expatriate Managers: Implications for Cross-Cultural Training Programs." *Columbia Journal of World Business*, 21, 1986.

_____. "The Dimensions of Expatriate Acculturation: A Review. " *Academy of Management Review*, 10, no. 1, 1985.

Middleton, John. "Vocational and Technical Education and Training. A World Bank Policy Paper." ERIC Document No. ED334454. A report by the International Bank for Reconstruction and Development, 1991.

_____. "World Bank Support for Vocational Education and Training: New Directions for the 1990s." *Journal Industrial Teacher Education*, Spring 1991.

Miller, E. L.; S. Beechler; B. Bhatt; and R. Nath. "The Relationship Between the Global Strategic Planning Process and the Human Resource Management Function." *Human Resource Planning*, 9, no.1, 1986.

Miller, Vincent A. *The Guidebook for International Trainers in Business and Industry*. New York: Van Nostrand Reinhold and ASTD, 1979.

Milliman, John; Mary A. Von Glinow; and Maria Nathan. "Organizational Life Cycles and Strategic International Human Resource Management in Multinational Companies: Implications for Congruence Theory." *The Academy of Management Review*, April 1991.

Misa, K. R., and J. M. Fabricatore. "Return on Investment of Overseas Personnel." *Financial Executive*, April, 1979.

Mitroff, Ian I. *Business Not as Usual*. San Francisco, CA: Jossey-Bass Publishers, 1987.

Montville, Joseph V. *Conflict and Peacemaking in Multiethnic Societies*. New York: Lexington Books, 1990.

Morgan, Gareth. *Riding the Waves of Change: Developing Managerial Competencies for a Turbulent World*. San Francisco, CA: Jossey-Bass, 1988.

Morgan, Patrick. "International HRM: Fact or Ficton?" *Personnel Administrator*, September 1986.

Morical, Keith, and Benhong Tsai. "Adapting Training for Other Cultures." *Training & Development*, April 1992.

Morris, Desmond. *Gestures*. London, England: Triad/Granada Press, 1981.

Moulton, Harper. "Executive Development and Education: An Evaluation." *Journal of Management Development*, 9, no. 4, 1991.

Murray, F. T., and A. H. Murray. "Global Managers for Global Businesses," *Sloan Management Review*, 27, no. 2, 1986.

Murray, Margo, et al., eds. "The 1992 Global Connector: The Complete Resource Directory for International Training & Development." Annual Directory of International Training Associations, Institutions, Societies, and Training and Consulting Firms, 1992.

Nadler, Leonard, ed. *The Handbook of Human Resource Development*. New York: John Wiley & Sons, 1984.

Nadler, Leonard, and Zeace Nadler. "Overcoming the Language Barrier." *Training & Development Journal*, June 1987.

Neale, Rosemary, and Richard Mindel. "Rigging Up Multicultural Teamworking." *Personnel Management*, January 1992.

Nelson, G. L. "The Implications of Schema Theory Reading Research to Technology Transfer in Developing Countries." In *Proceedings of the Human Factors Society—34th Annual Meeting*, 1990.

Noel, James L., and Ram Charan, "GE Brings Global Thinking to Light." *Training & Development*, June 1992.

O'Connor, Robert. "Britain Trains to Compete in a Unified Europe." *Personnel Journal*, May 1991.

————. "New Training Approaches for Europe '93." *Personnel Journal*, May 1992.

Oddou, Gary R. "Managing Your Expatriates: What the Successful Firms Do." *Human Resource Planning*, 1991.

O'Keefe, Bill. "Adopting Multimedia on a Global Scale." *Instruction Delivery Systems*, September/October, 1991.

Ogden, John D. "Designing Cross-Cultural Orientation Programs for Business." Ypsilanti, MI: Eastern Michigan University Report, 1988.

Ohmae, Kenichi. *The Borderless World*. New York: Harper Business Press, 1990.

Palmlund, Thord. "UNDP's Management Development Programme." *Journal of Management Development*, 1991.

Parry, Scott B. "Linking Training to the Business Plan." *Training & Development*, May 1991.

Peak, Martha H. "Developing an International Management Style." *Management Review*, February 1991.

Pedersen, Paul. *A Handbook for Developing Multicultural Awareness*. Alexandria, VA: American Association for Counseling and Development, 1988.

Phatak, A. V. *International Dimensions of Management* 2nd ed. Boston, MA: PWS-Kent Publishing Co., 1989.

Plihal, Jane, and Jeanette Daines. "How to Succeed in an Overseas Assignment." *Vocational Education Journal*. vol. 63, no. 3, April 1988.

Prahalad, C. K., and Yves Doz. *The Multinational Mission: Balancing Local Demands and Global Vision*. New York: Free Press, 1987.

Pucik, Vladimir. "Strategic Alliances, Organizational Learning, and Competitive Advantage: The HRM Agenda." *Human Resource Management,* Spring 1988.

Ralston, D. A.; D. J. Gustafson; P. M. Elsass; and R. H. Terpstra. "Eastern Values: A Comparison of Managers in the United States, Hong Kong, and the People's Republic of China." *Journal of Applied Psychology,* 77, no. 5, 1992.

Randolph, Benton. "When Going Global Isn't Enough." *Training,* August 1990.

Reich, Robert B. *The Work of Nations: Preparing Ourselves for 21st Century Capitalism.* New York: Alfred A. Knopf, 1991.

_____. "Who is Them?" *Harvard Business Review,* March-April 1991.

_____. "Who is Us?" *Harvard Business Review,* January-February 1990.

Rhinesmith, Stephen H. *A Manager's Guide to Globalization.* Homewood, IL: Business One Irwin, 1992.

_____. "Developing Intercultural Sensitivity." *Training & Culture Newsletter,* February/March, 1992.

_____. "Going Global from the Inside Out." *Training and Development,* November 1991.

_____. "An Agenda for Globalization," *Training & Development,* February 1991.

Rhinesmith, Stephen H.; John N. Williamson; David M. Ehlen; and Denise S. Maxwell. "Developing Leaders for a Global Enterprise." *Training and Development Journal,* April 1989.

Rhodeback, Melanie; Wen Ben-Lai; and Louis P. White. "Ethical Consideration in Organization Development: An Empirical Approach." *Organization Development Journal,* Winter 1990.

Ricks, David A. *Big Business Blunders: Mistakes in Multinational Marketing.* Homewood, IL: Dow Jones-Irwin, 1983.

Rigby, J. Malcolm. "The Challenge of Multinational Team Development." *Journal of Management Development.* vol. 6, no. 3, 1987.

Rimalower, George P. "Translation, Please." *Training & Development,* February 1992.

Rothwell, Sheila. "The Development of the International Manager." *Personnel Management,* January 1992.

San, Gee. "Enterprise Training in Taiwan: Results from the Vocational Training Needs Survey." *Economics of Education Review,* 1990.

Savich, Richard S., and Waymond Rodgers. "Assignments Overseas: Easing the Transition Before and After." *Personnel.* vol. 65, no. 8, August 1988.

Schleger, Peter R. "Making International Videos: An Odyssey." *Training & Development,* February 1992.

Schloss, Sylvia. "Training: From Lay-Bys to Languages." *Industrial Society,* June 1991.

Scullion, Hugh. "Why Companies Prefer to Use Expatriates." *Personnel Management,* November 1991.

Setliff, Rebecca J., and Lori A. Taft. "Intensive Language and Culture Orientation Program for Japan." Ypsilanti, MI: Eastern Michigan University Proceedings, 1988.

Shaeffer, Ruth G. "Building Global Teamwork for Growth and Survival." *The Conference Board Research Bulletin.* no. 228.

Sheth, Jagdish, and Golpira Eshghi, eds. *Global Human Resource Perspectives.* Cincinnati, OH: South-Western Publishing, 1989.

"SIETAR: Exploring Cultural Content." *HR Reporter,* vol. 6, no. 10, October 1989.

Silberman, M. *Active Training.* New York: Lexington Books, 1990.

Silvestre, Jean J. "Schooling and Vocational Training in Switzerland." *OECD Observer,* June/July 1991.

Singer, Marshall R. *Intercultural Communication: A Perceptual Approach.* New York: Prentice Hall (Simon & Shuster), 1987.

Snelbecker, G. E. "Practical Ways for Using Theories and Innovations to Improve Training." in George Piskurich, ed., *The ASTD Handbook of Instructional Technology,* New York: ASTD and McGraw-Hill, 1992.

Stacey, Ralph D. *Managing Chaos: Dynamic Business Strategies in an Unpredictable World.* London, England: Kogan Page, Ltd., 1992.

Steinberg, Carl. "Train in Vain?" *World Trade,* March 1992.

Stewart, Edward C., and Milton J. Bennett. rev.ed. *American Cultural Patterns: A Cross-Cultural Perspective.* Yarmouth, ME: Intercultural Press, 1991.

Stewart, Thomas A. "How to Manage in the Global Era." *Fortune,* January 15, 1990.

Stone, R. J. "Expatriate Selection and Failure." *Human Resource Planning,* 14, no. 1, 1991.

Storey, John. "Do the Japanese Make Better Managers?" *Personnel Management,* August 1991.

Stringer, Donna, and Linda Taylor. "Guidelines for Implementing Diversity Training." *Training & Culture Newsletter,* May 1991.

Stuart, Karen D. "Teens Play a Role in Moves Overseas." *Personnel Journal,* March 1992.

Stuart, Peggy. "Global Outlook Brings Good Things to GE Medical." *Personnel Journal,* June 1992.

Suzuki, Norihiko. "The Attributes of Japanese CEOs: Can They be Trained?" *Journal of Management Development* (UK). vol. 8, no. 4, 1989.

Swierczek, Fredric W. "Culture and Training: How Do They Play Away From Home?" *Training & Development Journal,* vol. 42, no. 11, November 1988.

Tachiki, Dennis S. "Japanese Management Going Transnational." *Journal for Quality and Participation,* December 1991.

"Taking the Cultural Blinkers Off." *Business Korea,* December 1991.

Taylor, Craig, and Fredric Frank. "Assessment Centers in Japan." *Training & Development Journal,* February 1988.

Taylor, William. "The Logic of Global Business: An Interview with ABB's Percy Barnevik." *Harvard Business Review,* March-April 1991.

Thiederman, Sondra. *Bridging Cultural Barriers for Corporate Success: How to Manage a Multicultural Workforce.* New York: Lexington Books, 1991.

_____. "Managing the Rainbow: Tips on Making it Work." *Cultural Diversity at Work*, November 1991.

Thurow, Lester. *Head to Head: The Coming Economic Battle Among Japan, Europe and America*. New York: William Morrow and Company, 1992.

Toffler, Alvin. *Powershift: Knowledge, Wealth and Violence at the Edge of the 21st Century*. New York: Bantam, 1990.

Torrington, Derek P.; Trevor Hitner; and David Knights. *Management and the Multi-Cultural Work Force*. Westmead, England: Gower, 1982.

"Training in the 90s: The Labour Force Development Strategy (Canada)." *Worklife Report*, 1991.

Treece, James B.; Karen L. Miller; and Richard A. Melcher. "The Partners." *Business Week*, February 10, 1992.

Tuller, Lawrence W. *Going Global*. Homewood, IL: Business One Irwin, 1991.

Tulving, E. "How Many Memory Systems Are There?" *American Psychologist*, 40, 1985.

Tung, Rosalie L. *The New Expatriates: Managing Human Resources Abroad*. New York: Ballinger Publishing, 1987.

_____. "Selection and Training of Personnel for Overseas Assignments." *Columbia Journal of World Business*, 16, no.1, 1981.

Tung, Rosalie L., and E. L. Miller. "Managing in the Twenty-First Century." *Management International Review*, 30, no. 1, 1990.

Vaill, Peter B. *Managing as a Performing Art: New Ideas for a World of Chaotic Change*. San Francisco, CA: Jossey-Bass, 1989.

Vance, C. M.; D. Boje; and H. D. Stage. "An Examination of the Cross-Cultural Transferability of Traditional Training Principles for Optimizing Individual Learning." Paper delivered at the International Conference of the Western Academy of Management, Shizuoka, Japan, 1990.

_____. "Global Management Education and Development: An Examination of the Cross-Cultural Applicability of Traditional Training Principles." Paper delivered at the National Conference of the Academy of Management, San Francisco, CA, 1990.

Vance, C. M., and M. Sailer. "A Glimpse of Human Resource Management Issues in Europe." In Mark Mendenhall and Gary R. Oddou, eds. *Cases and Readings in International Human Resource Management*. Boston, MA: PWS-Kent Publishing Co., 1990.

Volard, Sam V.; Dennis M. Francis; and Frank W. Wagner III. "Underperforming U.S. Expatriate Managers: A Study of Problems and Solutions," *Practising Manager* (Australia). vol. 8, no. 2, April 1988.

Wederspahn, Gary M. "Working With Interpreters." *Cultural Diversity at Work*, November 1991.

_____. "Cross-Cultural Services: Guidelines for Consumers." *Mobility*, January/February 1986.

Wedman, J. F., and M. Tessmer. "The Layers of Necessity ID Model." *Performance and Instruction*, 29, no. 41, April 1990.

Weeks, William H.; Paul B. Petersen; and Richard W. Brislin. eds. *A Manual of Structured Experiences for Cross-Cultural Learning*. Yarmouth, ME: Intercultural Press, 1985.

Weiler, Nick. "GE Strives to Develop New 'Boundaryless' Technical Leaders." *Training Directors Forum Newsletter*, April 1992.

Whalley, John, and Adrian Ziderman. "Financing Training in Developing Countries: The Role of Payroll Taxes." *Economics of Education Review*, 1990.

"Wharton Rewrites the Book on B-Schools." *Business Week*, May 13, 1991.

Wigglesworth, David C. *Bibliography of International Intercultural Literature*. Alexandria, VA: ASTD, 1989.

Williams, Gerald J. "The Key to Expatriate Success." *Training & Development Journal*, January 1990.

Wolniansky, Natalia. "International Training for Global Leadership." *Management Review*, May 1990.

"Workforce Quality: Perspectives from the U.S. and Japan. International Symposium." U.S. Department of Labor Proceedings, 1991.

Worthy, Ford S. "You Can't Grow if You Can't Manage." *Fortune*, June 3, 1991.

Wurzel, Jaime. *Toward Multiculturalism: Readings in Multicultural Education*. Yarmouth, ME: Intercultural Press, 1988.

Yamaguchii, Ikushi. "A Mechanism of Motivational Processes in a Chinese, Japanese and U.S. Multicultural Corporation: Presentation of 'a Contingent Motivational Model'." *Management Japan*, Autumn 1991.

Yankelovich, Daniel. "Tomorrow's Global Businesses." *The Futurist*, July-August 1991.

Yip, George S. *Total Global Strategy*. New York: Prentice Hall, Inc., 1992.

Zimpfer, Forest, and Robert Underwood. "The Status of International Business Communication Training in the 100 Largest Multinational United States Corporations." Ypsilanti, MI: Eastern Michigan University Report, 1989.

Index